C O

G4 Rev. 10/12cp

ANNE JORDAN

Zaccmedia

Published by Zaccmedia
www.zaccmedia.com
info@zaccmedia.com

Published May 2016

ISBN: 978-1-911211-27-3

British Library Cataloguing-in-Publication Data
A catalogue record for this book is available from the British Library.

ACKNOWLEDGEMENTS

Morning Has Broken, first published in 1931, was written by Eleanor Farjeon (1881–1965).

'The Lord's Prayer', version in this book taken from the *1928 Episcopal Book of Common Prayer.*

Excerpt from Winston Churchill's speech can be found at: http://www.theguardian.com/theguardian/2007/apr/20/greatspeeches1 (accessed 3.3.16).

PART ONE

CHAPTER
1

Outside the house, in the garden, the cat is busy digging in the frost glistening earth. Her eyes fix on small moving things. Night-time is the best time for hunting. She sits; wee water thaws a tiny patch of soil. She moves again and waits; a short distance away, a small creature smells danger...

Inside the house, two human beings are dreaming their private memories. The youngest one, Jimmy, wakes; his body is too heavy. He needs to find a hole. He must go to the bumwoodhole hoose. The poo plop is pushing his bottom out. He mustn't wake Grandma. She will not let him have the crust on the bread at breakfast if he does. He must be a good boy. He must walk on his toes.

He did his 'been' on the 'po' as a child, but he had played with its contents and wee and poo had been rubbed in three perfect circles on to the lino of his bedroom floor. It had been a good game but Grandma had been cross. She had grabbed him by the ear and frogmarched him to the netty at the bottom of the garden. Then she had showed him where to put his bum. He had liked putting his bum on a hole. She had also given

3

him some number word jobs to help him when he needed to go during the night.

Number one, get out of bed.

Number two, put his old coat on.

Number three, put his slippers on.

He will now count getting out of bed, as he always does, on his tall middle finger, then putting on his old coat on the next finger and, last of all, putting his slippers on, on his little finger. Then he has gone from biggest to smallest. This is always the right thing to do.

There are no sounds in the house as he goes downstairs to the kitchen, apart from the slow ticking of the mantelpiece clock in the front room. He pauses for a second; a strange smell is going up his nose. It's making his head feel a bit shaky. It's not the usual faint smell of bleach on the hard floor – put there to kill the cockroaches – or the spicy smell of leftover pease pudding. This smell is like rotten bird eggs he has smelt at the bottom of the bumpy giant tree in the garden, but there is no time to stop.

He opens the kitchen door and feels the cold outside air go down his throat and ice his chest. Now that he is outside he knows what will happen next: his toes will begin to move. Jimmy likes his toes as they always hit the ground before the rest of his feet. All he has to do is follow them. They are taking him towards the bumwoodhole. He must thump his feet down on the grass as he walks and clap his hands four times to frighten the goblins away. The cold air makes him want to do a wee too. He must hurry before it is too late, and get back to bed, where he can rub the warm air back into his toes.

He is almost there when a loud noise behind him, like a bomb going off, thuds through his ears and propels him skyward. For a moment he is in the sky. It is sparking with red darts. Then he falls. A sickening pain thunders through his head as it hits the top of the netty, then blackness. Jimmy is now lying unconscious on the ground.

Jimmy likes being Jimmy. He likes the village where he lives. He doesn't know it is called Hoxton and it is in Northumberland, but place names have no meaning to him. Jimmy is twenty. He is very proud of being twenty as it has a two in it, like the number of his feet. Jimmy knows nothing about the war which began last year. He has no idea it is the second world war of the century. He has no idea that people are calling it the phoney war. His hoose and its big coal fire are everything to him.

Hoxton is typical of the pit towns and villages in this part of the world, and the village has grown up around the mines. The arrangement is that a house and coal will be bestowed free in exchange for employment down the mines. Mined coal supplies an ever-thirsty country with power for its industries and railways. The work is hard and often dangerous.

Some miners who have worked down the mines for many years develop the miner's lung disease known as pneumoconiosis. This is caused by inhaling the coal dust in the mine. It is a slow killer which, among other symptoms, shows itself in shortness of breath. However, Hoxton's inhabitants are good-hearted, generous folk who accept their lot in life and look after their own.

Another thing Jimmy likes is his food; food fills his toes up and helps him to jump over the cracks in the pavement. He also has his own way of becoming your friend. If you want to be a friend of Jimmy's, you have to shake his hand three times. It's so that he can have a good look in your eyes to see if you are a good person or not.

5

Jimmy's favourite colour is purple, as it is the colour of plum jam. Red is the colour he dislikes most, as it is the colour of blood, which he is frightened of. When Jimmy has really sad word-thoughts in his mind they come as red. When Jimmy has really happy word-thoughts they come as purple.

Sometimes the words in his head move or sing. The singing comes into his head when he is happy. Sometimes he tries to speak the words but they don't always sound right to other people and that makes him sad. The only time people can sometimes understand him is when he sings. But he stopped singing when he went down with whooping cough as a child; because the coughs made him cry – and then he couldn't sing. So he jumps when he is happy – and when he understands what people say to him. He jumps really high when Grandma ruffles his hair.

Jimmy loves his Grandma very much. She is a canny, God-fearing lady who will give you her last crust; even if it is a bit claggy and has just a scrape of cheap marg spread on it. She is small and round-faced with wrinkles that arrived too soon; and her faded blue pinny loosens just a fraction more with every birthday.

Grandma knew very soon in Jimmy's life that he was 'different'. Some kids called him gormless and laughed at him but she had a sixth sense and knew when the bullying was going on. She would rap hard at grimy, mud-splattered windows and shake her stick at the even grimier offenders. That always sent the bullies scattering in all directions. Once, one of the bullies had gone away in a long box with handles, which Jimmy had seen some men carry to a big car. He wondered at the time why the bully's mar has been crying. The bully hadn't come back.

When Jimmy was little, the best thing he had in all the world was a sea-pirate book. He would climb on Grandma's knee and cuddle into her ample bosom as she read it. He liked the page with the picture of the fishes best. He would count them in turn, with his hand resting on their tails. There were always five. Grandma would make a wiggly fish shape with her arm and he would copy her. At the end he always looked to see where the sea ended – but the back of the book didn't have a picture of the end of the sea.

Jimmy grew up knowing no evil.

After what seems only a few moments, but in fact is a good twenty minutes, Jimmy opens his eyes. Why has he gone to sleep in the grass? It is cold and the frost-wet grass has wet his face, or maybe it is wee water – he doesn't know which. His bottom feels sloppy and his pyjama bottoms feel wet. He doesn't like that and Grandma hasn't come with some clean, dry ones.

He can hear voices but they seem far away. And there is a bad smell, which he can't put a name to right now. It is going up his nose and all around his body. He feels sick and his head hurts and the rest of him hurts and he wants to go back to sleep but the sleep song won't come. Instead, a red blood-dirge is filling his frightened mind:

Jimmy body not right.

But his body isn't ready to feel yet. The bad red song is now wobbling into darkness as once more he loses consciousness.

Meanwhile, at the front of the house, startled mining folk in family groups are fleeing their houses. A scrabble of arms grab coats and thick jackets and throw them around their night clothes. Dogs bark and a few stray cats flee the scene.

A swift-thinking resident from up the street has summoned the fire brigade. It arrives within minutes of being summoned. The police arrive and a young policeman, new to his job, begins the difficult task of keeping control of the growing crowd. His voice lacks the authority needed for the job.

'Get safely back, everyone. Move back.'

'But Jimmy and Grandma, they're in there.'

'The fire brigade are doing their best, madam. The ambulance will be here soon.'

A sudden moan goes out from someone in the crowd.

'Look! They've found Jimmy.'

'Stand back, everyone; stop pushing, please.'

It is hopeless, as everyone wants to see if Jimmy is alive.

'Look, they need to get him in the ambulance.'

'What about Grandma? Have they found her?'

'They're doing their best, madam,' replies the exasperated policeman. Father Keith, the local Catholic priest, arrives. He came the minute he heard about the explosion.

'Have they found them?'

'They've got Jimmy, he's alive, but I cannit tell if his injuries are bad or no. Found him by the netty, they did, lucky isn't the word. Who will have thought a trip to the netty could save your life? Don't know about the grandma, though. Sorry, but I must sort out all this pushing.'

Suddenly a communal moan spreads around those who can see what is happening. A body is being carried out on a stretcher; covered completely with a blanket.

'They've got her, Father. It's not good news.'

The policeman has returned to Father Keith to update him on recent developments. He pauses to regain his composure.

'The grandma – they've found her, but I reckon it's not a sight anyone should see. Terrible thing to have happened to a canny old lady, to die like that.'

Father Keith feels his stomach lurch.

'What do you think caused it?' It is his voice that now has the tremor.

'Well some folk thinks it was a war plane, but I reckon by the smell it's a gas fault, I divvin know for sure, though. There will have to be a proper investigation. There's debris up the road about 100 yards. Just as well next door is empty; that ceiling is hanging in a dodgy way, reckon they will have to knock it down. Yes, and we'll have to excavate a lot of people in the street!'

Father Keith tries not to smile at this unintentional malapropism. There is a war on, after all, and this accident has brought the noise of war into the village for the first time since the last one.

He thinks again about Grandma. She was a regular worshipper at morning services and Jimmy always accompanied her. Father Keith very quickly discovered that Jimmy was 'different', but he knows little about him and his background, and he needs to know more about him to be able to help him the best he can.

He will speak to Mrs Bailey. That will be the best option. She is a gossip – he knows that – and she knows everyone's business; but there is no helping it.

Anyway, the best thing now, he thinks, is to go home and try to get some sleep, if sleep will come.

It is a dismal morning in Hoxton when Father Keith turns the key in his door and begins his lonely walk to Mrs Bailey's house.

The curtains at the windows of every house he passes are closed, showing the usual respect for a death in the community. A dull Northumberland mining village looks even duller with empty pavements. It is as though a whole community has lost its sound.

He finds the house he is looking for and knocks on the door. It is a while before it is opened.

'Sorry, Father. Cum in and sit down. I've just shoved the bairns upstairs with some books to read. They're still scared but they're canny bairns, even though I says it meself; they won't be botherin us. Sorry to keep you waitin like that. I'm not thinking reet this morning.'

Mrs Bailey is a tall, thin woman who has kept her figure well. It is a credit to her, as she has delivered ten healthy babies to Mr Alfred Bailey, her husband, who is a village miner.

Alf, as he is known to his friends, is on the portly side and likes his bottle of dog just a little bit too much; but Newcastle Brown Ale keeps Alf going when screaming kids get on his nerves. Mrs Bailey is inclined to an 'it does me good' tipple herself.

Today, her thin face looks haggard as she ushers Father Keith into a sparsely furnished but clean front room. Father Keith takes in his surroundings as he sits down. The main bit of furniture in the room is a large oak sideboard which proudly displays an arrangement of different-sized photos of all the Bailey children at various stages of childhood. He is relieved to see that each brass photo frame shines with the results of regular polishing; at least Mrs Bailey isn't lazy, he thinks.

He decides to come quickly to the point of his visit.

'I've come to you, Mrs Bailey, because I know you will be able to tell me what I need to know about Jimmy.'

'Cup of tea, Father?'

'Oh yes, thank you.'

She scurries away to the kitchen and a few minutes later scurries back with the promised tea.

'Well, Father, I've knawn Jimmy as to when he were little, and then growing up in this grubby street with too many kids in it and not enough food for rumbling bellies and dads that work long shifts and mams that have too much washing.'

He nods; he knows what poverty means for a number of his parishioners. He suspects it will get worse with a new war to contend with.

Mrs Bailey continues with her story.

'Jimmy was small as a bairn, well, of course he still is, and that shock of black curly hair always reminds me of a shaggy dog and those big muscular arms like an ape, they were – are, I mean – it's them that make him strong. And then it's his eyes that you notice most about him. Right bonny eyes he's got, neither brown, nor green, but something in the middle with bonny long lashes and a clear way of looking at you and then he allers gets as close up to people so as he can look in their eyes. Not sure why he does that, though. Well, expect you've seen that already, Father.'

He nods again. He knows a little of what she is saying but doesn't let on; interrupting might make her go off-track. He has to exercise the patience he has learnt over years of being a priest!

'Some people find that a bit scary, but Jimmy will never do anyone any harm. He has a kind 'art, even as a bairn, and will do little jobs for you. And then he cannit talk right, either. And Jimmy loved his grandma even though she still treated him as a bairn, and she kept him out of Aggies – sorry, Father – St Agnes' House.'

Father Keith nods once more. He knows St Agnes' House, the local hospital for those classed as mentally deficient. Yes, Grandma has done well to keep Jimmy at home. St Agnes' House doesn't have a good reputation.

Mrs Bailey pauses for a second.

'And then...'

Father Keith rises from his chair. He has heard enough for one morning and the thought of Mrs Bailey starting again with 'and then' is something he definitely wants to avoid.

'Well, thank you Mrs Bailey, for your time. I really must ring St Mary's to see how Jimmy is.'

CHAPTER
2

St Mary's hospital is used to all kinds of people, having nursed a large number of patients since it was opened by the old Queen herself – but not one like Jimmy. By the sixth bed of a row of twelve, recently qualified Nurse Holmes is observing her patient. She has been checking on Jimmy every quarter of an hour and at last his eyes have begun to flicker.

Jimmy is now coming round. He is trying to open his eyes but finding it very difficult. It is as though an invisible enemy has ganged up against him and is pushing him back in to an unearthly darkness. But whoever the enemy is, he has not taken his hearing away, and the sounds he can hear are not the usual ones he hears when he wakes up in the morning.

Jimmy hear bad snoring.

Jimmy hear bad clicking.

Jimmy hear bad voices.

And all of these strange sounds are mashing together into a mess of noise. Jimmy can make nothing of it. Where is he and where are the noises coming from?

Jimmy's head hurt.

Jimmy not want to wake up.

Fortunately his body agrees with his head; it is too soon to know the answer to the mystery of why he is here.

And once more the world does not exist. It is just as well, as the memory of the gas explosion which has destroyed his house and killed his grandma will have been too much for his mind to take in.

It seems only a moment has passed when he next wakes. For a moment he wonders why his bedroom has become white and why there seems to be other people in it. Then his eyes begin to focus on the unfamiliar surroundings around him.

The shock to Jimmy's confused mind is immense. A visual overload of unfamiliar hospital objects runs towards him; beds with lying-down people, white walls, blue curtains, white ladies, chairs, jugs, bottles, pillows, cupboards and other strange objects that he does not know the names of begin to swirl in front of his eyes and then choke him. He can't breathe. He has to breathe. He has to open his mouth. He has to let the choke out.

Suddenly, the loudest shriek the hospital ward has heard in a long time surges out and propels itself through two uniform lines of hospital beds, stunning everyone with its force.

For a few moments the ward goes deathly silent then it relaxes again, glad that nothing has changed. Then out of all of it a white lady comes walking towards him. A soft voice speaks.

'It's alright Jimmy, you're in hospital.'

Nurse Holmes sits down on the chair beside the bed and puts her hand on his arm. This has a soothing effect and he turns his head to look closer at the white lady's eyes. They are good eyes and that makes him feel a bit better. He tries to think who the white lady is.

'Jimmy, do you know what I'm saying?'

He doesn't know what she is saying or why he is in hospital or even what hospital means. He has never been inside or visited anyone in hospital. It is a world he knows nothing about.

Fear, confusion and pain is all he can take in, and he continues staring like a frightened animal.

Then suddenly his mind can take no more. His mouth contorts into a half-human, half-animal shape and once more a shriek pushes its way out of his mouth and storms down the row of beds.

'Jimmy, you're...'

'Nurse Holmes, you need to give your patient a sedative.'

The sudden voice, belonging to Sister Stuart, who has appeared at the end of Jimmy's bed, stings the air around her with its cold efficiency.

'Yes, Sister, sorry, Sister. Jimmy, it's just a scratch on your arm, that's all.'

'Oh, stop messing around, let me do it.'

Jimmy isn't prepared for the pain of the hastily given injection. He moans at the intensity of it. He covers his head with his arms to stop the pain from spreading.

'That's done. Right, nurse, there are other patients to see to.'

'Yes, Sister.'

Jimmy's body heals quickly but his mind doesn't. He wakes each morning expecting to be back in his own home, but it just isn't happening. It is a desperate feeling; it has no music in it. Each day red blood whimpering words engulf themselves into hospital morning rituals.

Jimmy not at home.

Jimmy not at home.

Jimmy wants hug.

Jimmy want Grandma hug.

He thumps his bed each time to get rid of the words, but then the white lady always comes to him and she puts small things in his mouth. The small things slide in to his tummy and then he begins to feel floaty, like a kite.

Father Keith comes to see him too; he says nice words that he likes; some of the words he has heard in church when he has put his head down with the people. They have armen at the end of them. He doesn't know who the armen people are, but they must be nice as everyone looks up to see them.

He sometimes sees Father Keith looking sad. He wonders if Father Keith wants a hug from Grandma too.

In reality the sad face is hiding a troubled mind. Father Keith has no idea how to tell Jimmy that his grandma has died. He feels as a clergyman that he should be the one to do it. He is a man of the cloth, after all; it is his duty. After

16

much heart-searching taking a number of days, he decides to tell it simply; an idea has come in to his mind. He will say it tomorrow.

'Hello, Jimmy. How are you this morning?'

Father Keith's voice is quicker today. Jimmy wonders if it is because Father Keith is feeling sick. The cat was sick one day and she ran away from it.

Jimmy thinks maybe if he tries to speak, Father Keith won't run away.

'Ar reeet.'

He is pleased that his voice sounds like Jimmy's.

'That's good, Jimmy. Jimmy, you know when you come to church on Sundays...'

'Why aye, bonny lad.'

An unexpected voice behind Father Keith makes him jump and falter in his prepared speech. He has not heard Mrs Bailey's quick-light footsteps as she approaches Jimmy's bed. She has just arrived on the scene and is breathing heavily, having just found the right ward. Her thin face looks haggard and bags under her eyes shows she has not slept well the previous night. Her breath smells faintly of a 'little tipple'.

She dumps herself down in the seat opposite Father Keith, talking all the time. She had been awake a lot during the previous night wondering how to tell Jimmy about his grandma. Then the idea of the sea had come to her. She knows that Jimmy loved his sea-pirate book as a child, and that maybe he will understand that Grandma has died if she tells him that Grandma has gone there. After all, she has known Jimmy all his life. He has to be protected. Grandma has done it. She will do the same.

'Well, Jimmy pet, yer mist be teld reet now. Yer hoose has gone bang and yer grandma's gone beyond the sea! And I must be off now as it's me turn to do the flowers in chapel.'

Then she is gone, leaving behind her a mess of words to circulate in the air. Father Keith is both shocked and angry. He looks at Jimmy to see if there is any sign, or flicker, even, of understanding; but the eyes that stare back at him are blank and empty. The only option he has now is to pray for Jimmy; but what to pray for? He must bring calm back from chaos.

He will pray and return another day after he has done some more thinking.

His plan has been thwarted by a kind but thoughtless tipsy woman. Now, how is he going to get Jimmy to understand that his grandma has died, and also how is he going to undo the harm that has just happened? Where to begin? He has no idea.

He prays then leaves. He has a quick word with the nurse on the way out.

Jimmy is now beginning to think; his thinking is slow at first, but his mind has to carry on. He has to know what the words he has heard mean.

Jimmy HOOSE HOOSE gone bang. Beyond?

Jimmy thinks about the words 'gone bang'.

He waits for a picture to come in to his mind.

Slowly it comes, hard and piercing.

Jimmy knows, Jimmy knows it. BONFIRE NIGHT.

JIMMY'S HEAD sees BIG BANGS.

18

He did not like the bangs in the dark night. He put his hands over his ears. The bangs made him wonder where he was and they made him think the trees were coming to get him. Grandma had taken him home. He had been happy to get home and look at his sea-pirate book and fall asleep on Grandma's knee.

He likes the 'sea' word, though, but it doesn't go with the word 'bang'.

He thinks about the last word.

But the last word which has a 'b' sound makes no sense at all. He can only think of one other 'b 'word today and that is 'bed', but 'beyond' is a strange word. He has no idea what it means.

Then the words break rank and jumble up together in his mind like the memory of the kitten playing with Grandma's knitting wool. He had laughed at the kitten but Grandma had been cross and chased it away. But the kitten had stayed and its toes and legs had got big.

But now the fun has gone and the big bad words in his head are giving him a headache. All he can hear now in his mind are four red-coloured words.

Hoose bang. Hoose bang.

Has his hoose gone bang?

Has his hoose gone in to the sky?

His thinking is jerky but he can't remember seeing any fireworks. Maybe the hoose has gone with Grandma? He thinks some more about Grandma.

Grandma gone.

But why would Grandma go away?

19

At that moment fear walks through the hospital door again and, finding Jimmy, it bounds up the ward and grabs him by the toes. Then it shouts at him two, ice cold, red words:

Grandma gone.

Then it shouts loud in his head three more words:

Where   Where   Where

He puts his hands over his toes to stop the cold from spreading, but it is already working up his body. Three bad questions are coming into his mind:

Where is the hoose? Where is Grandma? Why have they left him?

He is holding his head on one side now to pour the questions out of his ears. He is very still. The bad questions are making his tummy go tight. A fear-snake has begun to move inside him, beginning at his cold toes, making them ache. It begins to travel up his stiffening body, its body twisting and contorting within its evil, icy path, engulfing him totally. It reaches his head with a hiss and fastens him to his bed. He opens his mouth and sicks it out. The nurse rushes to his bed.

CHAPTER
3

'Come in, Father, sit down.'

Father Keith has been summoned to the hospital early the next day by Sister Stuart. The phone call a short time ago has alarmed him. Her efficient voice has given nothing away. He is now wondering if anything serious has happened to Jimmy. He sits down and waits for her to speak.

She comes to the point straightaway.

'Jimmy Camm is upsetting the other patients. He keeps on crawling under people's beds as though he is looking for something.'

Father Keith frowns at this. The memory of the face of a silly talkative woman flashes in to his mind. The harm that Mrs Bailey may have caused is making him feel angry again. He tries to speak. However, Sister Stuart is not prepared to stop for any reason. She is determined to continue.

'And whenever he wants to go to the toilet, he jumps out of bed and then jumps again and I don't know how many times more, but you can guess how frightening that can be in the night when a patient is asleep.'

A sudden phone call interrupts her conversation. Her voice becomes sickly sweet when she realises it is the senior surgeon ringing about the progress of a difficult case. The call ends and Sister Stuart resumes her officious manner.

'Then he runs up to people on the way back, gets as close as he can, then stares in to their eyes, and he keeps on doing it. I have some very sick patients in my ward, Father.'

Once more she does not wait for Father Keith to reply. Any sympathy she may have had for Jimmy has disappeared. She has made her mind up about him and does not hesitate in speaking it.

'He will have to go to the asylum. There is a board meeting this morning. St Agnes' House is the best place for him. I've made my report and I have every confidence the board will agree with me. I need the bed too. There are old folk needing beds. It's this new flu virus. First it's flu, then pneumonia, and you know, Father, how it takes them, and some of my nurses are going down with it. The last thing I need is an idiot on my ward.'

Father Keith feels anger rising from his stomach. Where is Christian love or even tolerance in the woman he is looking at? he thinks. And yes, he does know how it takes them. He has buried a number of them already, and he has seen the despair in so many eyes.

But now, what to do about Jimmy? He has sensed that Jimmy will not survive in the asylum, despite his physical size. Grief will kill him. But what can he do to save him from a future at the madhouse? Father Keith is silent for a few moments. He is thinking about what Jimmy likes best in his life, next to Grandma, and then it comes to him.

'The lad needs a home.'

He sounds more confident than he feels, but he is used to handling all sorts of professional people, and stating the truth in his gentle but firm voice often produces results.

'He can stay with me for the time being, and my resident housekeeper, Mrs Coward, will take care of him. I will look around for something more permanent, maybe casual work.'

He isn't going to let them put Jimmy away. Not while he has anything to do with it.

'Well, I hope you know what you are taking on. He'll have to stay on his sedating medication. It might stabilise him after a while, but then you never know with these types when they might turn violent. But if that's what you want, well, good luck to you.'

Father Keith notes Sister Stuart's emphasis on the word 'might'. Yes, it is a risk – and he has no idea what he is going to do with Jimmy – but it is a risk he has to take. He has taken vows of Christian charity, vows which he has no intention of ever denying.

He tells Jimmy about the arrangement a few days later in the best way he can. Jimmy listens and accepts the idea. At least, that's what Father Keith thinks.

The reality is that Jimmy feels different lately. He doesn't know what the different feeling is. He can't put a name to it; all he knows is that his head feels funny, like it wants to go to sleep all the time. But there is only one thing he knows for certain: Grandma has gone. Can she be at the Father man's hoose? He must go and look. He must go and live there. He must look for her in the Father man's hoose and in the garden. He must find out about his hoose too.

And so he comes out of hospital and goes to live with Father Keith. And Hoxton carries on doing what it has always done despite a war which hasn't really impacted them.

House-proud wives continue to scrub their front door steps at the start of the day, knowing their knees will be dimpled and aching at the end of it. On washdays they sort out the washing into piles of whites and non-whites, ready to be boiled, mangled and hung out to dry. Skin-lined, moustached old ladies who live with their daughters continue to beguile each other over garden fences with the latest blather. Rosy-cheeked, unsophisticated young girls continue to make plans to go 'doon sooth' to get jobs as housemaids in big houses. And warm-hearted, cold-weathered old men, with lungs like coarse gravel, continue to hawk and spit green phlegm into cracked stone kitchen sinks. Life is still hard work for everyone, but there is always an escape at the pub, if only for a few hours.

However, for Jimmy, life is very different. He has a new bed to sleep in. It is not the same as the one he had in hospital. For one thing it doesn't move. It smells good, like flowers in church. But the best thing in his new bedroom is the clock on the wall. He likes clocks. They are round like holes and they make click-clap noises, like shoes on the ground when he walks.

But each day is making him feel more and more sad. Grandma and the hoose are not in the Father man's hoose. He had hoped they would be. He has looked under the bed and all the corners where things hide; and in the corners in the other rooms and under all the other beds. He has also looked in the pantry and the cupboard under the stairs. He has looked at all the outside places too. He is now running out of places to look.

The Father man had tried to get him to lie down but that had made him sleepy again. He has to keep looking; he has to stop the sleep from coming in to his eyes. He knows he must keep on looking.

Each new day he wakes up with the same urgent words going round in his head.

Jimmy find Grandma and hoose.

And he begins all over again to look in all the same places.

And then one day he wakes up and different words comes into his mind instead; and all at once in a fast line.

Jimmy's head hurt. Jimmy's arms hurt. Jimmy's legs hurt.

He tries to call for help, and after a number of tries help comes. Jimmy has flu. Whether he has picked it up whilst staying in hospital or whether it was afterwards no one knows. But it is no big surprise; hasn't half the street got it? And it is still taking lives. Father Keith suddenly finds himself very busy visiting the sick, some of whom are living in the parish hall, waiting for their homes to be repaired. The repairs are taking longer than expected.

The flu makes Jimmy feel very weak so Mrs Coward offers to 'nurse' him back to health. She calls it 'doing her Christian duty'. It is to help the good Father, to whom she is very loyal.

A few days later, just at the moment when she is about to begin a bit of spring cleaning, the doorbell rings.

'Oh, drat the bally thing.'

She makes her way reluctantly to the door and opens it. There stands Mrs Bailey, holding a bundle in her hand.

'Is Father Keith in?'

'No. He's out doing his sick visits.'

'Hope he doesn't go down with this flu.'

'Well, there is a lot of it about,' replies Mrs Coward in her matter-of-fact way.

'Well, I guess I can give them to you. It's a bundle of clothes. Reckon he must have lost all of them in the explosion. Jimmy, I mean. Well, course he has, poor lad. I've bin round the village and different folk have given what they can. And then, well, it's always the poor that looks after the poor. And…'

Mrs Coward knows Mrs Bailey very well, and her habit of starting everything with 'and then', so she is ready for the moment.

'Yes, I will make sure Father Keith gets them.'

It is a short but firm dismissal, and for once Mrs Bailey takes the hint. She goes without another word, feeling just a little offended at Mrs Coward's lack of conversation. Some people just don't want to have a good natter, she thinks to herself with righteous indignation.

The good Father is pleased with the clothes, but he is now feeling guilty that he hasn't told Jimmy about his grandma. Time has gone so quickly; but if he is honest with himself, he really doesn't know how to do it. It had been simple, he'd had a plan, but that was before Mrs Bailey put her two pennies worth in. However, he knows he can't tell Jimmy about Grandma while he has the flu. It would not be fair on the lad. He will have to wait until he is both strong in his mind and body.

It is the day before the funeral and Father Keith has woken up feeling exhausted. Fortunately, there have been no phone calls during breakfast to disturb him.

After breakfast is over, Mrs Coward walks with Jimmy to the parlour and helps him to sit down on a chair by the window. She tucks him in with a blanket and tells him not to go away. She has told him the same thing every day, but today she is very definite, as Father Keith wants to speak to him.

Jimmy has been glad of the chair during his recovery, as the parlour faces the front of the house and the chair is near to a window. He likes to watch people come up the winding drive of the house. Each time he catches sight of someone new he leans forward and puts his face to the window, hoping it will be Grandma. Sometimes he has fallen asleep with his face pressed against the windowpane. Some days have flown by, others have gone by very slowly. Each day the same plaintive question words frequently sting his sad, sore head.

Grandma coming to the Father man's hoose?

And he will try to call out her name.

But for some reason there is never anyone in the room when he calls out, no one ever hears his stressful plea, and his voice echoes back to him.

Today he will watch again and wait, but his waiting today is broken by a sudden voice.

'Hello, Jimmy.'

He flinches at the sudden voice but does not turn his head. He has forgotten that the Father man wants to talk to him.

Father Keith has decided it is time to tell Jimmy about Grandma. He has been so busy with visiting the sick, but he cannot put it off any longer.

'Hello, Jimmy,' he repeats gently. 'Jimmy, I must talk to you.'

He pulls a chair up and sits down.

This time Jimmy looks at Father Keith but then quickly changes his mind. He doesn't want to miss a moment of

27

looking out of the window. He has to keep looking; he might miss Grandma.

'Jimmy, look at me. It's important.'

He turns his head, trying his best to look out of the window at the same time. The effort makes him squint and he does not like it, so reluctantly he turns and faces Father Keith.

'You're looking better today, Jimmy.'

Jimmy likes the word 'better'. It has two good beats so he decides to have a go at saying it.

'ETTTER.'

Jimmy feels happy about how the word sounds. Maybe it is because he does feel better. He thinks about being better and what it means for him.

Jimmy head not hurting. Jimmy chest not hurting. Jimmy tummy not hurting.

Jimmy is a better boy now.

Jimmy smile for the Father man.

Father Keith absorbs the smile and is encouraged by it. Now is the time to speak.

'Jimmy, I am going to tell you about Gra...'

A sudden knock on the door stops him from continuing. Oh no, he thinks, please not now; then another knock, louder this time. He must answer it. Of all the times, must it be now.

'Sorry, Jimmy, I must answer the door.' He gets up out of his chair, goes to the door and opens it.

'What is it, Mrs Coward?'

'Sorry to disturb you, Father, but I have just had a message to say that Patty O'Hara has just given birth to a baby boy. It's come too soon; they don't think it will live long. She wants you to come and christen it.'

'Alright, tell her I'll be there as quick as I can.'

He knows Patty and her mother a little bit. He has seen them at the occasional morning mass when they have felt guilty about not coming very often. He is aware of Patty's reputation in the village. Lots of men climb the hill to meet Patty. She is liberal with her favours.

He turns and looks at Jimmy, but he has gone back to staring out of the window. Why this has to happen now, he thinks, just when he has summoned up the courage to speak…

'Sorry, Jimmy,' he apologises once more as he leaves the room. 'I really must go.'

Jimmy doesn't answer. He hasn't really listened that well to the words the Father man has been saying, and he has no idea who 'gra' is. He is now worried about the window. It has a wet bit on it which looks like a foggy day. He looks at his hands and finds his biggest finger to wipe the fog away. He doesn't want the fog to hide Grandma. He doesn't want to miss her coming for him. The fog has gone now and he can just see the Father man get in to his car. Maybe he is going to see 'gra', he thinks, and maybe 'gra' will give the Father man a mug of tea to warm his hands and toes when he gets there.

'Hello, Father, come on up.'

Father Keith has just arrived at the small cottage where Patty and her mother live, and has been let in. He nods to the midwife, who is now looking strained, and follows her to the winding stairs that lead off a small parlour. It is only a few steps to the bedroom where Patty is waiting. There is no Dada by her bed. Father Keith is not surprised by this, but thankfully the mother is here. She has not deserted her daughter, but a small frown crease in the centre of her forehead shows her sense of disapproval.

He cannot see all of Patty's lowered face, as a mass of tear-damp hair is plastering itself on her cheeks and on the thin cardigan hastily thrown around her shoulders.

There are no sounds in the room except intermittent dots of breaths coming from the tiny baby cradled in his mother's arms. Thank goodness he is not too late. He has done this before but it is never easy.

Patty looks up at the sound of Father's Keith's muted footsteps. Her red, swollen eyes against the ghost-white of her skin are showing the depth of suffering she is going through.

'Peace, my daughter. What name have you chosen for the child?'

'Joseph Peter O'Hara.'

It is barely a whisper, but Father Keith can just hear it. He mustn't make a mistake with the name. This is a tiny soul who will soon join the heavenly Father and the Holy Saints in heaven.

'It's time, my daughter.'

Father Keith cradles his hands around the tiny baby, and Patty releases her grip, and with one last kiss she places her son on Father Keith's waiting arms.

Father Keith dips two fingers in the holy water and gently strokes the sign of the cross on the baby's forehead.

'Joseph Peter O'Hara, I baptise you in the name of the Father and the Son and the Holy Spirit. Amen.'

'Amen.' The word echoes back from grief-lined lips and hushes the room. The dots of breaths are now miniscule. Father Keith hands the baby back to the mother. There is one sighed dot of breath, then stillness. He sees the midwife move to take the baby from the mother. He knows the crying will come again when he leaves. He has heard it so many times before, the desperate wail; the heaving sobs that stick to his feet on the stairs. He hears it again as he closes the door.

It is only a few steps to his waiting car, but each one feels heavy. It is the first war christening he has done. He wonders how many more fatherless war children he may have to christen in the years to come. The effect of the christening is battering his heart. Why is God allowing another war? He shudders at his own thinking. He is a Catholic priest, a man of faith; sometimes it's hard to have faith, he thinks; sometimes the unrighteous get a better deal in life. He shudders again. He mustn't have unbelief in his heart. He will say an extra two Hail Marys tonight.

And the day hasn't finished yet; there is the journey home and Jimmy to talk to.

He drives home with a heavy heart. He knows Mrs Coward will be waiting with a pot of newly boiled tea. She has a knack of knowing when a cuppa is needed.

'Thank you, Mrs Coward.'

The sweet, warm tea is very welcome to Father Keith's chilled body as he sits by the fire in the study. It's good to be out of the cold. He sips it slowly in the hope it will give him extra energy to speak to Jimmy.

31

'And just to let you know, Father, Jimmy has gone to bed. I found him asleep with his face pressed against the window. Guess it's all been too much for him.'

'Oh no, I mean, yes, he needs his rest.'

Father Keith tries to ignore the puzzled look which is appearing on Mrs Coward's face.

'Thank you for telling me,' he continues.

He sighs as Mrs Coward leaves the room.

CHAPTER
4

The next morning arrives slowly. Father Keith has slept badly and has been up in the night. He had tried to pray during his waking times about Jimmy, but his prayers had been laboured. Maybe he will be able to say the right thing to him today, but now he has no time to speak to him before the funeral. Jimmy has been too slow in getting up.

He feels bad about it. Perhaps Jimmy has come to understand what has happened to his house and to his grandma, he thinks. He doesn't really know for sure. It is a faint hope, but it is all he has.

He goes to his room to get robed and to prepare himself mentally for a funeral service. He will pray for Jimmy too, in the hope that he will understand what is happening.

Meanwhile, Jimmy has been told to put his coat on. Mrs Coward, the kind food nurse lady, has told him to fasten it up tightly. He has been told he is going to church. This is a surprise, as he usually goes to church on Sundays. He likes church, but what he really wants to do now is go to the window and look for Grandma. He must keep on looking.

But the curtains are closed today and he doesn't know why. He knows he has to do as he is told. Grandma always says so, and good words are coming into his head now so it must be alright.

Jimmy be a good boy.

Jimmy walk with the Father man.

Jimmy be a good boy.

Maybe Grandma wants him to go to church today, he thinks.

The village does its best to provide mourners for the funeral; those who survived the flu epidemic are there, but many are too ill to attend. The singing is strained but Jimmy isn't aware of it. A shiny picture on the window of some men fishing commands all his attention and drowns out everything else. He likes the picture as the men look happy.

After the service is over they assemble behind Father Keith and Jimmy, and begin to walk in silence towards the burial site. Jimmy likes the silence and he begins to walk on tiptoe. A purple lullaby song in his head surrounds him with tranquillity. Jimmy has always liked walking and he likes trees too. He wonders if everyone is going to climb them with him. That will make it a fun day.

Jimmy sees trees, hush trees.

Jimmy sees grass, hush grass.

The procession makes its lonely way alongside rows of burial plots: some of which have been the last resting place of those in the village who have died of Spanish Flu. The deadly virus which arrived in England after the Great War is a living memory for some of the older mourners. It took more lives than the war itself and devastated innocent families.

There are headstones which are elaborate, and some are over the top. But the saddest one of them all is a small grave bearing the simple inscription: '*Gentle Jesus meek and mild, Look upon a little child.*' *Our Grace, a much-loved daughter. May she know eternal peace.*

It belongs to Grace Woodhouse, aged six, the youngest victim of the Spanish Flu. It is guarded by a small angel who wears a sad expression as though it has known Grace personally. Jimmy looks at the angel as he walks past it. He has seen one before but cannot remember when. It makes him feel sad not to be able to remember. The sad feeling is making all the nice things smell funny like the air, the grass, the trees, and the people near him. He doesn't want to climb trees that smell funny.

Then suddenly everyone stops walking and the Father man says some words. They sound sad too.

The burial is a bleak affair. A pauper's burial with all that the word means. The mourners understand what is taking place. They feel the emotion of it all. They are saying goodbye to a life that has been a strong presence in their community. Grandma is no more.

Jimmy still understands nothing. He has seen boxes like the one he has seen today when he was a little boy and kids in the street had got ill and they had gone away in a box. He had thought it was because they were going somewhere to get better. That had made it alright.

But this is different. They have put the box in a hole and the Father man is saying more strange words. They still sound sad. The Father man is saying a name, Mrs Gladys James, and something about dust and ashes. He looks around him; he knows the word 'ashes', it is what you see when a fire stops being a fire. Outside fires always stop the music in his head; the fire might get big and chase him.

Jimmy not like fire.

He wonders if the Gladys lady has gone to make a fire. Again he wonders why he is here.

Maybe the eyes of all the mens and ladies will know.

The eyes will tell him. He will look at all the men's and ladies' eyes. So that is what he does. He has to stand on tiptoe to see some of them properly.

Jimmy sees closed eyes.

Jimmy sees down eyes.

Jimmy sees water eyes.

Some people pat his shoulder when he looks in their eyes. He has no idea why.

Jimmy doesn't know that a number of them are weeping silently at the unfairness of it all. The only bit left of a life well-lived is a plot number in the Catholic part of the cemetery. That is all there is.

Now they are walking back the way they came and the angel is still there. Jimmy wonders if her hands are cold as she is holding them together.

Then they go back to the Father man's house and the same sad people come too.

Then they eat sandwiches and sponge cake and drink tea in the big room. The same people pat him on the shoulder again. Some people say lots of long words he does not understand. Some just look at him and then turn away. Some just hurry past him and look down at the carpet. He has no idea why they are doing all of these things. Eventually they all go away.

He is now feeling exhausted. Maybe the Father man will let him go to bed. His legs feel heavy and his head feels too tight.

He walks to the slightly open window in the hope that some of the stuff in his head will fly away through the gap. It doesn't. So he bends down and looks at the legs of people walking away from the house. He likes legs. Maybe if he looks at the legs he will feel better.

Some of the legs are long with big feet. He likes big feet. Big feet can run fast like him. He doesn't know why the people were here today. He doesn't know why they are going away now. Most of all he still doesn't know where Grandma has gone. She has been gone a long time and he is missing her hugs.

Father Keith notices the weary expression on Jimmy's face and sits him down in an easy chair. Jimmy puts his head back in the hope that the sleepy feeling will drop out of his ears, but instead strange stripy shadows reflect the light from outside and make his eyes feel funny. He closes his eyes tightly to make it all go away, his face registering the utter confusion that is going on in his soul.

Father Keith sees the look on Jimmy's face and in an instant knows that Jimmy hasn't understood anything about what has happened to Grandma. Mrs Bailey's so-called kindness hasn't helped, and maybe has made things worse. Does the lad really understand anything at all about death? He has his doubts. Now is the time to speak. It has to be now. He takes a deep breath and seizing the moment, he begins.

'Jimmy, look at me. Jimmy, did you see an angel behind a stone today?'

Jimmy hear words. Words wake Jimmy up.

He must think.

Jimmy see a hole.

He must think some more. He must think; the red is hurting his head, but he must be a good boy today.

Jimmy see a box.

Jimmy see lots of eyes.

He thinks again, and then a good picture comes into his mind. He remembers eating cake. Yes that is it – angel cake. He has eaten angel cake. He can put a memory-face to angel cake. He will try to say it for the Father man.

'A g e l a k e.'

But, as always, the word does not sound right; it is always the same, the effort of trying to say words properly and then it all comes out wrong. It always makes him feel sad inside when people have to guess what he is saying. That feeling never goes away.

Father Keith has not understood Jimmy's answer. However, he is determined to keep going and tell him the truth.

He has been thinking of the statue of an angel behind one of the tombs in the cemetery and hopes that Jimmy remembers seeing it. It has been his plan all along to say that Grandma has gone to be with the angels in heaven. He remembers seeing Jimmy with his grandma at church at Christmas, looking at the nativity crib and pointing at the angel.

He also remembers hearing Grandma say that the angels live in heaven and one day she will go there.

'Jimmy, do you remember the angel at Christmas?'

Jimmy tries to think again. He must think for the Father man.

A memory, when was it?

Suddenly it comes back to him, the memory of Christmas. The pretty lady in the big box thing – he saw it with Grandma. He liked the pretty lady. She had wings like a bird. Grandma had said some words too but he had been too busy looking to see where the wings began on the angel's body. He has seen one today too when he went for a walk.

'Jimmy, Grandma has died; she is with the angels in heaven.'

Jimmy hears the words but they have no meaning. Maybe Grandma has gone to see the angel again, but why hasn't she come back? He wanted her to have some angel cake. Grandma likes angel cake. He must think.

He is feeling desperately tired but somehow he knows he has to think. The silence is palpable but Father Keith in his wisdom knows not to end it. He prays silently and in that same moment Jimmy's mind clears, a purple happy memory 'behind song' sings to him.

Jimmy knows the word 'behind'. Jimmy know the word 'behind'. Good boy, Jimmy. Jimmy knows it.

He had often hidden behind the curtains when playing hide-and-seek with Grandma when he was little. The hiding game had been fun, just like holes had been fun. He thinks some more but the words will not go purple. He wants them to go purple and they begin to go that colour but now they have changed. The red has come and got bigger and made them stop.

Jimmy not know the word 'died', not know the word 'heaven'.

JIMMY HEAD HURT.

Suddenly he feels sick, very sick. Mrs Bailey's words and Father Keith's words and the red and purple colours are mashing together into a hopeless swirl in his mind.

Then something new happens. Four words begin to grow out of all the words he has heard about where Grandma has gone. They get bigger and dance together in a circle and then they sing a new four-word song. Then they put themselves in a line. And he does not feel sick any more and the words make sense and they sing a beautiful new purple song.

Grandma – behind – the – sea.

GRANDMA – BEHIND – THE – SEA.

Then something stupendous happens. This is the moment when he knows what he has to do next. He has to look for Grandma, who is with the hoose, behind the sea. It is easy and Jimmy feels a wave of understanding fill his face. And Father Keith sees it too and feels at last that Jimmy has understood him.

But the wave is fleeting and flickers away completely. New red words are now arriving in Jimmy's head.

Jimmy not know how to get to the sea.

Jimmy – think.

Jimmy looks down at his wide chunky feet as though they will have the answer. Then a sudden sense of loneliness comes over him and he begins to cry.

Jimmy water in eyes.

Jimmy neck wet.

JIMMY SHOUTING IN HIS HEAD. JIMMY FIND THE SEA.

THE SEA, THE SEA, THE SEA.

Father Keith, seeing the flood of grief, feels relieved that at last Jimmy has finally understood about death. His heart loosens in him.

Jimmy, however, is now drowning in unknown waters. And the water is carrying him away to somewhere he has not yet been. Somewhere he has yet to find: the sea; but how is he going to do it?

More important than that, where does he begin?

CHAPTER
5

Father Keith has slept badly again. It has been the same all week. Thoughts of 'will Jimmy cope with casual work, especially now there is a war on?' have been dominating both his daytime and night-time thinking. But the alternative, an institution, horrifies him. He needs to get out of the house and think. He will do his thinking walk, to a place he knows well which has picturesque views over the local Northumberland countryside. He will go now. The peace and quiet may clear his mind.

It doesn't take him long to get to what he calls his memory bridge. This is his haven. He has stood on it many times, simply watching the flowing water in the river below. He has seen its many changes, often coinciding with the seasons, but today it is gentle. Now, as he looks into the clear water a memory of himself playing a merry game of Poohsticks comes in to his mind.

He had pretended to be a child and had watched the sticks being churned around in the fast-moving water. He had been entranced by the sight of silver trout darting their way downstream. It had been a peaceful morning. But then a sense that the peace could not last had spoilt it. For the first time he had felt a gut-sickening feeling that something bad was coming. He had been right.

It was only a few weeks later when the bad arrived. He had been in the pulpit, a bright Sunday morning in church, and instead of preaching a sermon he had heard Chamberlain's stark, factual speech from a crackly wireless declaring that *'Britain and France are at war with Germany following the invasion of Poland two days ago'*.

That is when it had first begun. That is when he had looked into the eyes of his congregation and seen icy communal fear inject each worshipper in turn. The peace negotiations had failed. Chamberlain was a broken man. War had come to Great Britain once again. He had been devastated.

Today he feels just as bad as he did then. A vulnerable young man's future depends on him.

He walks home with the same questions with which he had set out.

Two days later, Eddy Woodhouse the local farmer, decides he has to ask Father Keith a question.

Eddy Woodhouse is a small man in his early forties, with thick, unruly curly ginger hair and a rough beard. Eddy has the sort of personality that everyone likes. When he laughs, his round face brightens and his eyes sparkle. He liked the new parish priest right from the beginning, and the two men have formed a respectful friendship.

Today he looks purposeful as he sits opposite Father Keith in his study. Father Keith can't help but notice that his good friend looks a little tired and just a bit older than the last time they spoke. However, he says nothing; probably just war-weariness, he thinks.

Eddy clears his throat and begins to speak.

'It's this, Father. I've just been to the village hall with some eggs for the Young Wives and, well – to cut a long story short, they're wondering if the pancake race will go ahead this year. Some of them are saying it's a shame for the kids not to have it and it might cheer people up a bit, especially after what's happened.'

'Yes, why not. Let's give the children something to look forward to.'

'Glad you agree, Father.'

'Well, now, how about some tea and some of Mrs Coward's homemade scones?'

'Thank you, Father, don't mind if I do, and if you don't mind me saying, Father, you look dog-tired.'

'Do I? Well, it's – no, I'll just get us some tea first, then I'll tell you why.'

Tea and scones go down a treat. Eddy waits for Father Keith to continue his story. Father Keith then begins again.

'Now, Eddy, I'll tell you what's on my mind. It's Jimmy Camm. I just don't know what to do about him.'

Eddy nods sympathetically.

Encouraged by Eddy's nod, Father Keith gives an accurate account of everything concerning Jimmy's welfare.

Eddy listens without interrupting and nods at opportune moments. Despite not having a brilliant education, he has the gift of grasping problems quickly. Suddenly a solution to the problem enters his mind.

'I've got an idea, Father, but I need to put it past the missus first. I'll tell you all about it after the race. Yes, that's the best idea.'

45

'Well, any idea is better than nothing. You coming today has been a blessing, I can tell you. I've been at my wits' end, not knowing what to do for the best.'

'That's OK, Father, glad to be of help.'

After Eddy has gone, Father Keith helps himself to a small glass of port. The port does the trick; within a few minutes he is fast asleep in his chair. He dreams of tossing a thick pancake at a troublesome parishioner!

The morning of the pancake race is fortunately fair, with a small chance that the sun may shine later.

Father Keith has been asked to start the race and Eddy Woodhouse is positioned at the finishing line – just before the road takes a left turn into a much narrower road. Jimmy is there at the finishing line too, seated on a garden chair, wrapped in a blanket. Father Keith thinks it might be fun for him to be there and watch the race.

'Now, children, the rules are the same as last year. You must not drop your frying pan. Remember, you have to flip your pancake four times in the air during the race and catch it again. You little ones, you toss the pancake twice.'

'That means two times, do you hear?' called out a fussy mother.

'Yes, quite so,' continues Father Keith. 'You will have four pancakes each, so if you lose one it won't matter. The first one past the finishing line with a pancake in the pan is the winner.'

The race begins and the first group sprint away down the High Street towards the finishing line. Then the second group does the same. Finally, it is the turn of the last and eldest of the teams to begin.

They are off. Pancakes are flipped and lost. Many are trampled on and some stick to the soles of the children's shoes. There is much laughter; a welcome change from the previous solemn days.

It looks as though there is going to be a clear winner. A long-legged lad of about ten years old is tearing towards the finishing line. The crowd begins to roar. He is going to win, but just as the winning line comes in view he trips over a pothole in the road and goes sprawling near to where Jimmy is sitting. A communal 'Oh no!' spreads in the crowd. The clear winner has lost and another runner wins the race. But for Jimmy the lost race is doing something in his head, a memory is stabbing him. What is it? What is it? It's exciting, he wants to jump. He must jump.

Jimmy jump.

He jumps and feels the air around him rush through his ears. Now two good purple words in his head are beginning to sing. He jumps again.

Jimmy go.

The singing is telling him something and it is making his toes and feet want to move. He jumps again.

JIMMY GO.

'Hey, look at Jimmy!' someone cries out from the crowd. 'He's pinching the frying pan and running off with it.'

A picture has come in to Jimmy's mind. It has come from the sky and it is growing bigger; a picture of when he was little: running, splashing, getting wet...

Jimmy run.

JIMMY KNOWS THE SEA.

Jimmy run to the sea.

He must run.

He must run to the sea!

Voices call out urging him to stop but Jimmy keeps going. Adrenaline pumps into his weak legs and forces him onwards. Only Jimmy knows where he is running to; no one else does. And his happy song keeps on singing.

JIMMY FIND THE SEA.

He is running like a rabbit fleeing from a farmer's gun: away from the village and the noise of shouting people; away from the houses and the shops and the churches and away to his memory.

Out of breath now, he slows down until his steps become plods. Each foot feels heavier than the other with every new step, but his body will not let him stop. And then he sees what he has remembered.

JIMMY LOOK. JIMMY LOOK. JIMMY LOOK.

It is the big water he ran in as a child; clear and long, running down to who knows where, tumbling over itself, splashing its merry way and purposefully carrying its own kind. This must be it. This must be the sea. Why has no one told him that it is the sea?

This is the water he has put in empty jam jars and carried home. There were tiny wiggly things in it, but they hadn't

48

looked like the fish in his sea book. But they moved and that made him laugh. Then one day the wiggly things were sleeping on the top of the water and he had shook the jar to wake them up and they hadn't woke up, so he had gone out to play cat holes.

And now the happy song is getting happier by the minute.

THE SEA.

JIMMY FINDS THE SEA.

He stops running and sinks down on his knees on the riverbank. The mid-March earth feels cold through his clothes and his head hurts but his body feels hot. Something is banging hard in his chest, and all the water on his tongue has gone away.

But he knows what he has to do; all the words come jerkily in to his head in one purple rush. The last word jumps higher than the others and the song jumps too.

GRANDMA

BEHIND THE

WATER.

The water is hiding Grandma and that's why he can't see her; just as she has been behind the curtain in the hide-and-seek game. All he has to do is find her behind the seawater and the hoose will be there too. The song becomes a march.

JIMMY MOVE THE WATER.

He feels energy go into his arms.

JIMMY MAKE A HOLE IN THE WATER.

He begins to dig at the water with the frying pan. Then it becomes a swirl and begins to fly. He feels dizzy and exhilarated all at the same time. Then the dizzy feeling spreads all over his body and the sky begins to move sideways and he can feel the wet soil slide up his legs. Then he feels his breakfast come up into his mouth and it tastes all wrong. That is when the song stops as always happens when the red words come.

JIMMY'S EYES GOING ROUND AND ROUND.

JIMMY'S HEAD GOING ROUND AND ROUND.

JIMMY'S EYES GOING BLACK...

CHAPTER

6

Geoff Harrison is feeling happy with himself. He has just finished his round of delivering letters to the waiting people of Hoxton. However, there is one more delivery to do; the last of the morning. It is a parcel for the farm, addressed to Eddy, and it looks important.

He enjoys his postman job and he whistles as he drives along the narrow farm road towards Low Mill Farm, which is situated two miles away from the village.

He takes in the scene as he guides his van around the rough bits of the road. Forsythia bushes show off their individual shades of yellow and contrast expertly with the emerging fresh green of new spring grass. For a moment a sense of the numinous fills his soul and he feels that he is one with nature. The war seems far away today.

Delivering to the farm is always a pleasure for Geoff. It means a chat with Mary, who everyone says is a bonny lass, and the added pleasure of a freshly cooked bacon sandwich.

There had been a time when he had walked out with Mary Whiting. Mary was – and still is – beautiful. She is slim but not skinny, with enough curves to attract any number of Geordie lads. Her hair, which she wears to her shoulders, is titian with a tint of golden brown. It curls into her neck, framing her high-browed face with the stately look of a medieval maiden. Her wide, innocent eyes hide a shrewd personality. She has a well-rounded nose and her smile widens a dimple in her left cheek. But Mary isn't vain and she never flirted or giggled her way into anyone's heart. It is Eddy Woodhouse Mary has fallen for, and Geoff has bowed to the inevitable.

She married Eddy and fourteen years later they are still happy. Their only sadness has been the lack of children. It just hasn't happened. So Mary has compensated by being the best wife she can be. She also practises counting her blessings as her devout, deceased parents taught her to.

Geoff continues along the road. It is an easy journey as there is no other traffic about. He arrives at the farm in good time and parks the van outside the farmhouse entrance. He jumps out of the van and is greeted by Snap the farm dog.

'Come on, Snap, let's find your mar.'

However, Mar has heard the noise and is already standing at the farmhouse door, waiting for him.

'Morning, Geoff, and it's a bright one, better than yesterday, it stotted down all day up here.'

'Same in the village. I blame Hitler,' replies Geoff with a shrug of the shoulders.

'Reckon he will ruin our weather if he can. I've got a bad feeling about this new war. Anyway, come in, kettle's on.'

Geoff doesn't have to be asked twice. He knows that 'kettle's on' also means a bacon sandwich. The thought of Mary's homemade bread with lashings of crispy farm bacon has keep him going along the road.

One bacon sandwich and a large mug of tea later and Geoff is ready for conversation.

'How's Eddy?'

Mary doesn't answer. Lately Eddy seems – well, it is difficult to define. There is something not quite right, but she just doesn't know what it is. Geoff notices the frown that has suddenly appeared on Mary's face so decides to change the subject.

'Gather you've got Jimmy Camm with you here. Do we know yet why he took off like that?'

'No idea. Eddy found him by the river; you know, the bit near the waterfall.'

'Oh, I know where you mean; just before it does that sharp right-hand curve and then goes out of sight.'

'Yes, and he was still holding that frying pan in his hand. But goodness knows what he was trying to do. There were little puddles of water next to him and he was soaking wet. The doctor said he had fainted.'

'I'm not surprised, seeing the way he ran off like that.'

'Yes. Tell you what, though, he's strong. That's why Eddy thought about having him up here at the farm. And seeing him run the way he did at the race just confirmed it.'

'And you, with your kind heart, said yes straightaway.'

'Something like that.'

'You always did have a kind heart, Mary Woodhouse.'

'Jimmy's in bed now. The doctor gave him a strong sedative.'

'So what are you going to do with him?'

'Reckon Eddy will have something in mind. Who knows, Jimmy might turn out to be good at doing farm jobs. And he can stay at the cottage and have his meals up here with us. We'll give it a try, anyway. We need all the help we can get.'

53

'Drat this bally war. It's the young lads who always suffer most. There was enough killing in the last one. I know.'

'Yes, and I guess there will be those who are just as keen as they were to join up. I reckon Ian will go soon.'

'When you say Ian, do you mean Ian Mitchell? Is he old enough to join up?' asks Geoff.

'Well, he'll be eighteen soon, April, I think, so he might be off with the rest of them.' Geoff doesn't reply; there is something about Ian that he doesn't like. What is it about him? Never puts a foot wrong, but then he once saw a snarl on Ian's face when he thought no one was looking and it made him wonder.

However, he doesn't say anything to Mary. He will never upset her, not for anything, especially today when she is looking more tired than usual.

He wants to ask her if everything is alright. If only she had been his, he would have taken her into his arms; but she isn't and that is that. Instead he speaks in a light-hearted voice: 'We're both very quiet this morning. Guess this war's got our tongues, and I've gone and forgotten to give you your parcel. I've left it in the van.'

They laugh together and the kitchen fills with spring light. Geoff goes out to get the parcel for Mary.

Meanwhile, upstairs, Jimmy has just woken up after a very long sleep. He opens his eyes and looks around him. He has no idea why he is in a strange hoose and not at the Father man's hoose. Yet he doesn't feel frightened. The sedative is still doing its work.

He is in a strange bedroom; it is very quiet, but it is beautiful and it smells of plums before they are made into jam. He feels strangely calm and floaty and light. He feels as though his head is walking in the sunshine and his feet are jumping in the soft blanket clouds. A strange sort of peace is filling him up and he feels he is in a good place. Maybe Grandma and the hoose are here. He did not find them at the Father man's hoose or at the wiggly-things water. He must look.

But first of all he has to get up and do all his usual getting-up jobs, but Grandma isn't here to help him and he needs to go to the bumwoodhole and he hasn't been told to go outside. He tries a few door handles and looks in but there is no bumwoodhole. He tries another and finds a bumwoodhole in it. He likes this room because it smells nice and it has bum paper that looks soft. And it has purple curtains at the window. He has a go at a wash but he cannot see when he closes his eyes so he washes his fingers and hopes the water will go inside his body and wash the rest of him.

Now to go downstairs and find out where the windows are so he can look for Grandma.

At the bottom of the stairs he stands for a while looking around him. The hall he is in is very big and has lots of doors. He does not know which one to open so he tries the first one as he likes the shape of the door knob.

It leads into a pleasant study with lots of books and a big desk and big plates on a shelf on a wall. He likes the plates. They are nice round shapes and remind him of holes. He looks at them for a long time, then he comes out of the room and closes the door. He chooses another door because it has a big crack in the wood. He likes the crack because it looks like the wiggly things he has brought home from the big water.

This door leads in to a front parlour. He has never seen anything so nice-looking before. It makes him feel as though he

55

is in church and he should be quiet like Grandma used to say. His eyes scan the room, taking in every detail. There is so much to see and his Jimmy-song is becoming quiet and melodic.

Jimmy look at the hush hoose.

He looks at the walls and counts the pictures. There are five of them and they all have different people in them. He walks up to them in turn and scans their eyes. They have good eyes, like the people in the very big windows at church.

Jimmy hush for the good people.

He turns around and is just about to bend down to see if the settee feet have toes when the door suddenly opens, making him jump, and the song jumps with him.

'Oh, here you are, Jimmy. I thought it was you I could hear.'

Jimmy hears nice words.

Then the song climbs up again and sings cheerful words to him.

Jimmy sees smiling lady.

Then it sings it again with a happy jump.

Jimmy sees happy lady.

'My name is Mary, Jimmy.'

Jimmy hears two names, Mary-Jimmy.

He has not met a Mary-Jimmy before. But it makes him feel happy that the nice lady has a name like his.

'Sit down, Jimmy pet, and I'll tell you why you're here.'

Jimmy do it.

'Jimmy, you have come to live on a farm.'

Jimmy in a farm.

Jimmy find Grandma in a farm.

The sea in a farm?

'Jimmy, if you come to the window, you can see the farm.'

Jimmy do it.

'If you stand here you can see the farm.'

Jimmy do it.

Jimmy sees lots of hooses.

But best of all there is lots of soil. Soil is good; it keep his feet from falling over. He can see soil now from the window. It is there in the fields and it has lots of different browns in it, as Grandma's eyes are. And there is so much of it. It goes all the way up to the sky.

The soil makes him remember a song that Grandma used to sing to him when he was little. He was small enough to sit on her knee and he had looked directly at her face, watching her lips move. He had liked how the sunshine had lightened her dark-brown eyes as the sunshine came and went, making them different colours.

And now the words of the song are arranging themselves in order and making sense.

Jimmy knows it.

Jimmy knows Hold hackonald.

Then to his surprise he begins to sing.

> *Hold hackonald ad a arrm E-I-E-I-O!*
> *And on at arrm he has sum hicks, E-I-E-I-O!*
> *ith a cuk cuk eer and a cuk cuk are*
> *eer a cuk are a cuk*
> *eggywhere a cuk cuk*
> *Hold hackonald ad a arrm E-I-E-I-O.*

Mary laughs but it is not an unkind laugh. And she is amazed that when Jimmy sings she can understand his words.

'Yes, we have chicks, Jimmy. They are in the hen house.'

She points to the hen house.

Jimmy continues with his song, and at the end of the verses he knows, Mary points in the direction of where that animal lives. Eventually he comes to the last verse.

> *Hold hackonald ad a arrm E-I-E-I-O!*
> *And on at arrm he has sum ucks E-I-E-I-O!*
> *ith a qwak qwak eer and a qwak qwak are*
> *eer a qwak are a qwak*
> *eggywhere a qwak qwak*
> *Hold hackonald ad a arrm E-I-E-I-O.*

He is so happy he has been able to sing that he jumps into the air four times. He has remembered the old man song and he has been able to sing it. The cough hasn't taken the singing away!

By now Mary is so moved by listening to Jimmy sing and the realisation that he remembers all the words from childhood that she cannot speak immediately. But more importantly he actually sang it for her; and that is special. Blinking her tears away, she replies in her best controlled voice, 'Yes, we have ducks, Jimmy. You can see the duck pond from here.'

He strains to see where the Mary-Jimmy lady is pointing. And yes, he can see a duck and the duck is on the water and then suddenly the E I E I O music in his head takes on some new words.

Jimmy look at the duck. E-I-E-I-O.

Jimmy sees the water. E-I-E-I-O.

Then a traffic jam of words form themselves into an exciting queue in his head and become a strong purple song, and the song sounds in his head like this:

THE DUCK IS ON THE WATER.

LOTS OF WATER.

WATER ON THE BIG HOLE.

LOTS AND LOTS OF WATER.

Then the words grow in his mind and become even more exciting. He begins to jump up and down and the purple words got really big and the song gets louder in his head.

A BIG BIG HOLE.

BIGGER THAN THE WIGGLY WATER.

That is it, he has found the sea. The pancake one hadn't been right but this sea hole is bigger than the pancake one. This one must be the sea. It has to be! A new exciting song jumps in his head. He has found the sea!

GRANDMA and the hoose.

BEHIND THE DUCK WATER SEA.

He tries to sing the words but because they are so exciting they do not want to leave his head, and all that comes out is a gurgling sound. Mary ignores the gurgling sound. She thinks it the polite thing to do.

Instead, she waits patiently until he stops jumping. She isn't really sure how to react to him, but at least there hasn't been any challenging behaviour to deal with. She watches to see what he will do next.

Unlike at the pancake race, Jimmy doesn't move. He wants to move but suddenly he is feeling very tired and his head feels heavy and he wants to put it in a bed. Jimmy knows the sea is big and now he has found it on the farm. He will start looking at it the next day. The song is now hushing him to sleep.

Jimmy have a rest now.

He gives a big yawn.

'ARRRR.'

Then he walks up to the settee, curls up on it, and soon is fast asleep.

At the end of the day, Mary, now tucked up in bed, reflects on how the day has been. It has been a good start. Tomorrow she will show him the cottage, and hopefully Eddy will be able to give him some useful work to do the following day. It is all going well.

The next morning finds Jimmy much better than he has felt for a long time. It is a greyish morning with the possibility of rain later on, but the grey clouds that hang down from the sky do not worry him. He has woken with a hazy memory of the previous day. A picture of the Mary-Jimmy lady and a song about the farm man floats into his head and settles into a good place in his brain. Then all the things he has done rush through his ears in a purple running line.

He is happy about them all.

Then the memory of the duck sea joins the Mary-Jimmy memory and they cuddle up to each other. After that comes the exciting memory. Today is going to be the day he will find Grandma and the hoose. Today is going to be the love day. Today is going to be the best day of his life. He has eaten his breakfast and the Mary-Jimmy lady is now smiling at him.

'You're looking much better today, Jimmy.'

He likes the word 'better'. It makes a song that sounds like this:

Jim me bet ter. Bet ter.

Jimmy say better for the Mary-Jimmy lady.

'Etar.'

The better song suddenly comes to an abrupt end.

Jimmy not happy with saying better.

The better song starts again and it is telling him what to do.

Jimmy try again.

'Eter.'
The better song comes to an abrupt end once more.

Jimmy not happy with saying better.

The better song starts again.
'ETTUR.'
This time it is louder and clearer.

Jimmy now happy with saying better.

Jimmy smile at the Mary-Jimmy lady.

Mary, seeing the elongated mouth smile, takes it as a clue to continue speaking. She is feeling her way a bit with her attempts at communicating with him.

'Today we are going to see the cottage where you will live.'

Jimmy looks confused; he doesn't know the word 'cottage' and the singing is not helping him. He wants to start looking for Grandma immediately, but Grandma has always told him he must do all his little morning jobs before anything else. But it still doesn't make sense. Mary notes the confused look on Jimmy's face.

'It's like a house, um, a hoose,' she explains.

Jimmy is happy. He is going to live in a hoose while he looks for Grandma and his own hoose. He is so happy that he claps four times.

'And tomorrow Eddy will show you what to do.'

Jimmy thinks that sounds good too. Maybe the Eddy man will help him dig the new water. He feels very happy indeed so he gives a big-mouth grin and claps three times. It is a day he has found singing again, so he claps another three claps.

'Put your coat on, Jimmy, and we can walk to the cottage, I mean hoose, now.'

He is happy about putting his coat on and he is happy about the new purple jobs-to-do song that has come into his head.

Jimmy walk with the Mary-Jimmy lady.

Jimmy walk to the hoose.

Jimmy sees lots of things.

Jimmy like new farm things.

Jimmy likes red thing with big mouth.

There are new smells too. Strong smells such as pig muck, hay, hard labour sweat and a blend of animal aromas mix together in his nose.

Jimmy keep walking.

And now the smell is changing. It is earthy with spring freshness. He likes the new smell. It smells like the cat sometimes smelt when it had gone missing for a few days.

And now the sweeping views of green and brown fields lie before him. His eyes film it all. It is his. It is his new farm world.

But best of all is the sight of the duck sea. It is still there. It is waiting for him. He is so happy that he jumps lots of times as he walks and the fresh air makes big circles round his body and he feels more alive than he has done for a long time. His strong arms feel light. His feet feel as if he is dancing in cotton wool.

Mary feels content too as she guides him towards what is going to be his future home. A few minutes later they are there.

'Here we are, Jimmy.'

Jimmy suddenly stops jumping. The hoose where he is going to live is in front of him. It is glorious sight, so glorious in fact that he bends his body forward and stares at the hoose with wide-open eyes. He just can't believe what he is seeing. The sight of the farm cottage with its pale pink stucco front is the most beautiful thing he has ever seen. It stands on a low hill with a clear view of the farm. There is a small but neat garden at the front which is split in two by a stone path leading from a wooden gate. The trees surrounding it all bend towards it as though they want to be a part of its magic. It is a cottage where you can imagine love rules. This is a home for good people. Nothing bad can ever survive in this enchanted spot.

'Jimmy, this is where you will live.'

Jimmy love cottage hoose.

Jimmy go in to cottage hoose.

The first thing Jimmy notices inside the cottage is that all the walls are not straight. They seem to slope towards him as if they are giving him a big cuddle. He wants to cuddle it back.

Jimmy give big cuddle to cottage hoose.

Jimmy put cuddle arms on the walls.

Jimmy likes big hoose cuddle.

They go upstairs.

'Jimmy, this is your bedroom.'

The first thing Jimmy notices is the bed. It is in the centre of the room, covered with a big, thick, dark-green eiderdown.

He sits on it and feels the green colour.

It feels strong.

He feels the white sticking-out bit of the pillow.

It feels gentle.

He feels the rich golden brown of the carpet under the bed.

It feels like the cat had felt; smooth and long.

It all feels very good and he is very happy with his bedroom. He gives a big, wide grin. The grin shows a bit of bread on his teeth that he is going to swallow later.

Mary sees the excitement on his face and understands it as Jimmy being pleased with the new house.

'Yes, Jimmy, it's all for you.'

He wants to say thank you because that is what Grandma has taught him to say when someone does something for him. So he has a go at saying it but it doesn't sound the same as it does in his head. His tongue keeps getting in the way.

Mary doesn't understand the words that Jimmy is trying to say but she smiles. She doesn't want to spoil the moment by asking him to repeat what he has just said. Then she sees his eyes fill up.

Jimmy has seen the all-too familiar not-understanding-Jimmy look. He feels upset so he pushes his head down on his chest to stop the crying from coming up to his head. But then he realises he really doesn't want to cry as he is having such a good day. So he pushes his head back up again and grabs hold of Mary's hand and shakes it with a big up and down movement. In his head he can hear a purple gentle lady song.

Jimmy like the Mary-Jimmy lady. Jimmy like the Mary-Jimmy lady.

He has not felt this way about anyone except Grandma. It is a good, happy, innocent feeling.

And this time there is water in Mary eyes and Jimmy sees it.

And as Mary hugs Jimmy, their tears mingle together and become one. Out of the blue, Jimmy feels love again and Mary discovers for the first time what it is like to be a mother. It is a while before she can speak but it doesn't matter. Jimmy doesn't mind; he now wants to look for the window. His eyes search the room. Then he finds it. It is there, big and wide inside a cuddle wall. He walks to the window and looks all around it. It is a good window. It is big enough to get all of Grandma in it. He will be able to see her. It is a very good window indeed.

'Jimmy, look at me now. I want to see your face.'

Mary has seen the wonder in Jimmy's eyes but knows she has to speak of more practical matters.

'Jimmy, you will sleep here, but you will have your breakfast at the farm and a nurse lady who the doctor knows will come in the morning and bedtime to help you.'

She waits to see if Jimmy has understood.

'Is that alright, Jimmy?'

He knows it is alright because a good purple word sings in his mind.

Yes.

It is such a good word that he decides to say it.

'EeSS.'

And it sounds right and he is so happy he jumps three high jumps.

Today is a day when he has liked lots of words that have been said to him, but the word 'breakfast' has been his favourite. He has always liked breakfast. Grandma used to make porridge and he would sometimes put a large dollop of plum jam on it at Christmas. And he likes the idea of a nurse lady coming. He liked the nurse lady in hospital; that is the one who sat with him and talked nice words.

He says his special word again because he is feeling especially happy.

'EeSS.'

'Jimmy, you will also have dinner at the farm.'

He knows about dinner too. Grandma made big stews with anything she could find and cooked it slowly for hours.

They tasted wonderful and filled him up from toe to head.

He makes another noise from his mouth; the same as last time which Mary understands to be yet another yes.

'In the middle of the day you will have sandwiches which I will give you at breakfast-time,' continues Mary.

This pleases him very much and a purple, happy-feeling, three-word song comes into his mind and sings it twice, getting faster all the time.

Jimmy like dinner. Jimmy like sandwiches. Jimmy like dinner. Jimmy like sandwiches...

Jimmy is so happy he does his happy jumps again. He has met the Eddy man and the Mary-Jimmy lady and seen his new cottage hoose.

Most of all he has seen his new window.

During all of this time, a few miles away a young farm labourer is beginning his journey back to Hoxton after visiting his granddad. The old man died unexpectedly while his grandson was staying with him, leaving him a tidy bit of money. He will be arriving any day soon.

CHAPTER
7

Mary is feeling very pleased with everything so far. Jimmy has seen the cottage and has walked back with her to the farm. He was quiet and thoughtful and she had wondered if he had been overawed by everything.

The sensation of wonder and joy at being a part of something special had taken her by surprise. She has always understood life in a certain way, the way she is expected to see it. Jimmy has taken her into his world. It has been a revelation.

But now the important thing to do is have something to eat. All the effort of the morning has left her feeling hungry. She has been feeling increasingly hungry recently. She has put it down to the war; why the war she doesn't know, but the war is getting blamed for everything these days. They will have sandwiches with her homemade bread and their own farm ham. She gets everything out of the pantry and begins to make them. She also tells Jimmy to wash his hands in the sink and sit down at the kitchen table.

Jimmy does as he is told and then sits down to wait for his sandwiches. And what sandwiches they are! He can hardly believe what he is seeing. They look different from any sandwich he has ever seen. They are chunky and full of something he cannot identify. And in his head two good purple food sentences slosh around excitedly.

Jimmy sees sandwiches. Jimmy eat the sandwiches.

He takes the plate and takes a bite from the middle of a sandwich. The bread is different from the sort Grandma used to make sandwiches with. For one thing it has holes in it, and the middle has more holes than the outside. He wonders what the holes will taste like. He puts his tongue in one of the holes. The edges of the holes crumble and melt onto his tongue. It feels good. Then he swallows big bits of sandwich without chewing first. This is fun. He can feel all the holes going down his throat. The meat inside the sandwich makes him want to sing; he has never tasted anything so good. It is even better than the plum jam in plum jam sandwiches. It is so good that he wants all of his mouth to feel the wonderful taste.

Jimmy push all the sandwich in his mouth.

Jimmy eat the next one.

Jimmy push all the sandwiches…

'No, Jimmy no. One at a time or you'll make yourself sick.'

Jimmy listen to the Mary-Jimmy lady.

Jimmy stop eating now.

Jimmy not want to be sick. Jimmy not like sick.

70

'Drink some tea, Jimmy.'

That is good, he thinks. That will stop the sick from coming.

Jimmy drink tea for the Mary-Jimmy lady.

Jimmy does not gulp the tea, but sips it in a series of three sips at a time until it is completely empty. He then hands the mug to Mary and claps three times. It has been a happy food time. She takes the mug and the empty sandwich plate and puts them in the sink. Jimmy laughs and claps at the disappearing plate and mug and then looks at his feet. He is glad that the food has gone all the way down to his toes to make him strong again. He is glad too that the good purple food song has sung to him.

Meanwhile, Mary is wondering what to do next with Jimmy. There is just one afternoon to fill before Eddy starts working with him tomorrow. Turning to face him, she looks directly into his eyes and speaks very slowly and clearly.

'What shall we do now, Jimmy?'

Jimmy doesn't reply. He doesn't know how to. He wants to go to the duck water but he doesn't know how to say it. Mary realises what she has done; she has expected Jimmy to answer a question. Why has she done that when she has been doing so well? But then she notices Jimmy's face begin to contort with strange sideways movements. He is trying to speak!

'Qwakorker.'

'Sorry, Jimmy, can you say that...' she stops herself from finishing the sentence.

She is doing it again. Her own crossness with herself shows on her face. Jimmy sees it and thinks it is because he is making a mess of things; but he has to try again. Grandma will want him to.

71

'Qwa orker.'

Again it doesn't sound right, but he has to keep on trying. He so much wants to tell the Mary-Jimmy lady he wants to look for Grandma at the duck water, but he cannot find the words. He waits but the words are stuck in his throat. But then, unexpectedly, six important purple Jimmy do-it words come into his head in a line. They come with a picture of the farm song he has sung with the Mary-Jimmy lady.

Jimmy sing the duck water bit.

And he begins to sing the duck bit of the farm song; only louder this time and with more excitement in his voice. Mary joins in with the chorus and they sing raucously together. Instinctively, Mary knows Jimmy is trying to tell her something about the ducks. Then suddenly she knows what it is.

'Jimmy, would you like to feed the ducks with me?'

Jimmy likes the idea of the ducks having some food, but what he really wants to do is find Grandma. But then, the Mary-Jimmy lady can feed the ducks while he looks for Grandma, he thinks.

It is such a good idea that he jumps three high jumps and claps his hands three times. The jumps do the trick and Mary scurries off to find some stale bread. It only takes her a few moments to find some. And now all she has to do is put it in a bag and then for both of them to put their coats on and they are ready. She waits for Jimmy to come back from the toilet, then shutting the kitchen door they set off together in the direction of the duck pond.

The walk takes them past a number of thick bushes which look like giant mushrooms. Jimmy feels safe walking next to them, as they make him think about a knitted brown hat he once had. He had made six holes in it by pushing his little finger in the knitting gaps. The holes had got bigger and he had wiggled his fingers through them and onto his head. He had enjoyed twirling his fingers around his thick hair and pulling it tight.

The next things he sees are two egg-shaped puddles with some of the water taken out; the early spring sun has dried it away at the edges. The dried bits make him think of Grandma's stew when it overcooked and stuck to the big enamel pan. As he walks past the puddles he looks to see if there are any orange carrot bits in it – but there aren't. That doesn't worry him as the next thing he notices are two tall trees which are very close together. He wonders if they are trying to tickle each other.

This makes him think about the time when Grandma tickled him under the arms. He wonders if the trees are ticklish too. He wants to jump up and tickle each leaf in turn, but he is suddenly stopped in his tracks by the biggest and best hole he has ever seen. And a big-hole purple chant begins to beat time in his head.

Big hole water. Big hole water.

BIG BIG HOLE WATER.

Good hole water. Good hole water. Good, good hole water.

From where he can see, the big sea hole is full to the top. And it is the most exciting water he has ever seen. It is clear, deep and reflective, possessing its own life. Its shimmering silver-green and light blue colours are enchanting. It has trees and bushes and grass in it. The sky is in it too and moving clouds go down in it and it is glorious and wonderful and happy and serious all at the same time.

And it feels as if his eyes will burst with ecstasy. A sense of awe stills his body and mind and he can do nothing but stare at the scene a little way in front of him. And a heart-water song swishes and splashes in his soul.

Jimmy look. Jimmy sees the sea hole.

Mary also stands still, sensing that he needs some looking time, and waits patiently until he is ready to move again. But Jimmy is still in a state of reverie and the heart-water song now has some new words.

Jimmy look for Grandma in the duck sea.

'Jimmy, shall we find the ducks now?' prompts Mary.
No reply or movement.
'Jimmy, the ducks are just around the corner.'
Jimmy remains still, his body absorbing energy from the power-force around him. Then suddenly his legs become strong like iron, they release him and he leaps forwards like a runner at the beginning of a race. He sprints towards the water which he believes is the sea, and every step he runs says three good words in his head. The words get quicker and louder and very bright purple and more and more melodic the nearer he gets to the water's edge.

Jimmy go to sea. Jimmy go to sea. Jimmy go to sea.

And the last three words pound his whole body, blotting out every other noise around him, even the frantic calls from Mary.

They are the biggest and purplish words he has seen; and the loudest song he has heard.

JIMMY FIND GRANDMA.

With his heart pounding with excitement, he arrives at the duck pond. Mary is still running behind Jimmy, but he has no awareness of her. The world has shrunk down to a kaleidoscope of water. And the water is still silver and green and light blue and has trees and bushes and grass and the sky in it and moving clouds going down in it, but they have grown bigger and are making a new world. For Jimmy it is a behind-the-sea world where Grandma is; a world he wants to go to. A good jumping song urges him forward.

Jimmy jump in the water. Jimmy jump high down.

Jimmy jump down to the top of the tree.

Mary cries out for him to stop. But he either can't hear her or is just not listening. Then to her horror she sees him lean forward, arch his arms and jump into its icy depths.

It takes a few moments for his body to react to a sudden drop in temperature. Then it does. Cold, brain-numbing, skin-freezing water surrounds his skin and shoots a knife-like pain in to every pore and tissue. It makes him gasp for breath. For a moment he does not know why he is there. Then he surfaces, but the shock has taken all his strength and his mouth is full of dirty pond debris.

Mary is very frightened. She knows how cold the water is in March and although her instinct is to jump in after him, she knows the danger of doing so.

'Jimmy, get out of the water.'

Jimmy hears bad words from the sky.

He cannot make sense of the words. Why is the sky talking to him and why is there no singing in his head?

Fortunately for Mary, he has jumped close to the water's edge.

'Jimmy, kick your legs.'

No reply.

'Jimmy, can you hear me?'

At that moment the sky becomes a person and a face he knows: it is the Mary-Jimmy lady.

'Jimmy, you must kick your legs.'

Jimmy legs not move.

Mary, sensing that Jimmy cannot move his legs, tries a different tactic.

'Jimmy, grass, move arms?'

Jimmy arms not move.

Again there is no movement.

'Jimmy, you must put your arms on the grass.'

This time the words arrange themselves in the right order

Jimmy arms must move, move for the Mary Jimmy lady.

'Put one arm out then the other.'

Jimmy do it.

'Now the other.'

Jimmy do it.

'That's good Jimmy now grab my legs and push your body up.'

Jimmy do it.

'Well done Jimmy, you've made it.'

To Mary's relief Jimmy is breathing, albeit shallowly, but he is very cold and white. She quickly undoes her coat and wraps it around his body, scooping him upright at the same time. Together, rescuer and rescued stumble their way back to the cottage. At times, Jimmy stops, very out of breath; and he trembles constantly; but eventually the cottage comes into sight. Mary, mustering all the energy she has left, manages to get him inside and into the kitchen.

The next few hours are spent getting him dry, into bed and getting some of Eddy's old clothes for him to wear when he wakes up. She copes with all this in her calm, efficient way, despite still feeing shocked by the whole incident. She also manages to get herself dry. Then, feeling utterly exhausted, she falls asleep in the chair next to his bed.

She awakes with a start about two hours later. For a second she wonders where she is, then the events of the afternoon come back to her with a sickening thud.

A whirling of questions shrieks at her from different directions and flood her mind. Why has Jimmy behaved in such a bizarre way when he was so happy earlier?

Is this a delayed reaction, or the beginning of some horrible breakdown caused by the grief of losing his grandma? If so, will they have to let him go? And then where? Like everyone in the area, Mary knows about Aggies. She shudders at the thought of him ending up there. Once in, you never get out.

No, she thinks, better just to let him sleep and let the nurse give him something to eat when he wakes up. She will bring down some food from the farm. And after dinner she will have a chat with Eddy, if he is in a chatting mood. She will have to be tactful; after all, there might be a good reason why Jimmy has behaved as he has. She must think about what to say to her husband.

CHAPTER
8

'So, why is Jimmy not here, then?'

Eddy has been patient and has waited until their evening meal is over. Mary has promised she will explain everything once they have finished eating.

'I took him down to the duck pond this afternoon to feed the ducks – after showing him round the cottage – and to cut a long story short, he did something very strange.'

'How do you mean?'

Mary feels relieved that Eddy sounds his usual self again.

'Well, just as we got near to the pond he suddenly shot off as though he had ants in his pants.'

She then tells him about the strange events of the afternoon.

After she finishes, she waits for Eddy to reply. He is usually able to grasp a problem quickly and come up with a solution; if not there and then, at least within a short time.

In reality, he is just as puzzled as Mary.

'Sounds a bit like the pancake episode; water and all that.'

'Yes, you're right, it's similar,' replies Mary.

'Look, pet, its early days and we need to get to know Jimmy. The lad's had a big shock and who knows what's going on in his mind.'

'Well, I suppose so; but it worries me a bit and, well, I just don't know...'

Mary has a frown in her reply and Eddy is quick to notice it.

'Look, I've been thinking about tomorrow, and this is what I think might work.'

Mary's frown goes a little at the possibility that Eddy has come up with something.

'I have decided to let Jimmy help me with building the Anderson shelter. I won't give him too much to do after what happened today...'

'Oh, I thought you were going to get Ian to do that when he came back from visiting his granddad.'

'I was, but I reckon I'll give Ian the usual March jobs to do. He knows the ropes, Jimmy doesn't. There's certainly a lot to do now that we're short on labour. Can't expect too much from Jimmy after what happened today.'

'What exactly is an Anderson shelter anyway?' enquired Mary.

'Well, my love, it's...' He is about to explain what an Anderson shelter is when he is suddenly aware of how especially beautiful Mary is looking tonight. Her eyes hold a tenderness which is compelling. Her slightly parted lips are full. Her curves are inviting.

She is all he has ever wanted. She has bewitched him. She is his and no one will take her away from him.

He notices her slightly rounded stomach and wonders if she has put on a bit of weight. If so, it suits her. He wants to hold her and make her his. He wants to own her always and forever and away from any harm that war might do. He has to protect her. The Anderson shelter will do that. They will go in there together and love will keep them safe. He bends forward and takes hold of her hand. He kisses it gently.

'Hey you, now, none of that, you've got that look on your face, Eddy Woodhouse!' laughs Mary. 'You're supposed to be telling me what an Anderson shelter is, and there is something I want to tell you.'

Mary's teasing rebuke brings Eddy back to the present. He laughs out loud. His wife has the knack that a lot of women have of reading their spouse's mind.

'Alright, you gorgeous creature, chase you later! Serious stuff first. An Anderson shelter is a place you go to if there's any bombing. You make it with steel panels and the end panel has a door in it. Then you bury it in the ground and put soil and turf on top.'

'And you think Jimmy will cope with all that?'

'Yes, why not? He can hold the panels for me when I bolt them together. That's not too hard, is it?'

'Well, you know best when it comes to the farm stuff, but...'

Mary's voice trails away. Eddy is looking tense again and his voice has sharpened. She had noticed the look on Geoff's face when he had come with the parcel and they had spoken about Ian. Will Ian be happy about the changed workload? Is there something about him that Geoff has seen but Eddy is oblivious of? She suddenly feels uneasy. The talk can wait. It can wait until Eddy is in a relaxed mood.

The following morning Jimmy wakes up with muscle aches in his arms and also some in his legs; but his heart aches even more than the rest of him put together. The events of the previous day had played out in his dreams which kept them alive with poignant power. He has not found Grandma. It has all gone badly wrong. He has to try again; this he knows with all of his innocent heart. How he intends to go about it, he has no idea. However, he is hungry, and breakfast has to come next, after the nurse lady has been.

Breakfast has always been a hearty affair at the farm, and the war has not yet diminished its supply of fresh food. There is bacon with deep golden-yolk eggs and large chunks of homemade bread and, most important of all, plum jam made with last year's fruit harvest.

He eats the eggs first as they have good yellow sunshine in them. Then he eats the bacon, cutting each piece lengthways so it will be the right size to fill his toes. A large mug of steaming hot tea follows and he drinks all of it down to the last drop so that his toes will feel warm. He now feels much better.

After breakfast is over, Mary gives Eddy a pack-up of sandwiches and a flask of tea for them both. Jimmy watches as Eddy puts them into a large bag. He then turns to Jimmy and speaks.

'Jimmy, I have an important job for you to do.'

Jimmy knows he has to do as he is told. But he is happy about it as he knows there will be plenty of time left in the day to find Grandma.

'Right, lad, I want you to help me build a very special house. It's because there's a war on.'

Jimmy hear three new words.

But what do they mean? He understands that he has to do something but he can't see anything in front of him. He begins to feel anxious. He needs to see what he has to do and the words are not helping him to understand.

Jimmy not know build.

Jimmy not know special.

Jimmy not know waron.

These are strange red words. He thinks about the last word, as it is the last one he has heard.

Maybe the waron is like the lion which he has seen in a picture book as a child and Grandma had told him was like a big cat. If it is a cat then he might be able to make holes with it in the garden. If that is true, then it is good to know about the waron. Maybe when he has found Grandma, he will play with the waron. The word grows bigger and bigger and bursts in his head and it becomes a happier word.

Waron. Waron. Waron. Waron.

Then six song words in his mind arrange themselves together and make sense. Then he realises that house is hoose. Eddy says hoose in the same way as the Father man says it: house. It had sounded strange the first time he heard it said that way, but now he understands it. And now they are going to make a hoose for the waron.

A hoose for the big waron.

He begins to dance for joy. Happy noises come out of his mouth and Eddy smiles at Mary. It is a reassuring smile that says there is no need to worry now. She smiles back, but it is a smile with an 'I hope so' look in it. He has seen that kind of smile before but today he is willing to believe that everything is alright. It is a new day and a new start.

'And I also want you to meet Ian. He works for me. He is about your age so I hope you two will be good friends. He will be here soon.'

Jimmy wonders if the Ian man likes holes. Maybe the Ian man has seen the waron. He thinks about the waron again. Will it be bigger than the cat, and will it be able to jump really high? Maybe they can jump together. A new purple waron-jump chant drums in his mind.

Jimmy jump with waron. Jimmy jump with waron.

And best of all, Ian might help him find Grandma. And just when he is about to clap a happy-Jimmy-waron-Ian clap, Ian arrives.

Eddy has always taken Ian at face value. He is a man of few words but never rude, and even though he often looks glum, Eddy thinks it is just the way he is.

He has also been impressed with Ian's timekeeping, which never alters, and the way in which he always asks after Mary's health if she isn't there. And he always does what he is told to do without any grumblings. There is no doubt about it – the lad works hard and hardly has a day off with so-called illness. Eddy has never liked shirking. He has built the farm up to be what it is today, and hard work has paid dividends. He wonders why Mary has been less enthusiastic about Ian. There are times when he thinks Mary is too sensitive about things. Maybe it is the lack of children in their lives.

Eddy looks at the two men who now stand in his kitchen waiting for him to tell them what to do, and is struck by how different they look from each other.

Ian is tall and thin with a long, thin nose. His high arched eyebrows make him look as if everything in life is a surprise to him. His dark-blond hair is cut very short and adds to an already long forehead. His way of standing with his head turned to one side of his body adds to the surprised look he already has. It is as though he is constantly thinking about something and is then surprised at his own ingenuity. Eddy wonders for a moment what sort of things Ian thinks about; but then stops. This isn't the time for procrastination.

'Jimmy, this is Ian.'

Jimmy shake hands with the Ian man. Jimmy shake hands with the Ian man.

Ian takes his time in offering Jimmy his hand, which turns out to be the grubby end of four fingers, and gives him a limp handshake, avoiding eye contact. Eddy does not notice the limp handshake as he has turned to walk towards Mary to kiss her goodbye.

Jimmy suddenly feels a coldness creep up from his toes to his head. He has to know if the Ian man is good or bad. There is only one way to find out if the Ian man is good or bad. He has to look at the Ian man's eyes. He knows he will have to stand on his toes to do so, so this is what he does – but it is doomed to failure; Ian simply turns his head away.

Jimmy is now feeling very anxious. He can't tell if the Ian man is good or bad. He really has to know. So he tries again.

This time, Ian, seeing Eddy's eyes on him, obliges and allows himself to be stared at. But there is nothing there; neither goodness nor badness – and that is disturbing.

For Jimmy it is the first time in his life he has seen something different from good and bad, and he doesn't know what it is and it makes him feel mixed up. And he doesn't want to jump or clap or be happy; he doesn't know what to do. He feels as if all his energy has gone out of his body and his senses are telling him something is wrong. There is no one to show him what to do as the Eddy man has just left the kitchen to find the anderdon instruckshun sheet. Jimmy wonders if this is for the Eddy man's bed.

He looks down at his toes in the hope they will show him what to do. They don't, so he looks up and sees Ian grinning at him.

For a moment Jimmy thinks that Ian is going to be friendly. But is it chance or accident that he suddenly feels a big ouch on his toes?

Jimmy feel Ian man foot on Jimmy's foot.

Jimmy foot squashed in the floor.

He is so surprised at the sudden pain that he doesn't cry out. He is thinking too hard about his toes and wondering if they will run again.

The action is hard, swift and done with. Ian then moves deftly to the window just in time for when Eddy returns to the kitchen, having found what he is looking for.

Jimmy doesn't know what to do. The last time someone hurt him was when he was a child and Grandma had sorted it out. But now there is no one to sort the hurt out and no time to count his toes as the Eddy man is speaking.

'Alright lads, let's go and I'll tell you what I want you to do as we're walking.'

Jimmy is glad the Eddy man has said that; it will give him chance to see if his toes will work. He follows him out of the kitchen and wiggles all his toes in his shoes as he walks. He is glad his toes are still working. And a good toe-wiggling song sings to him in his head.

Jimmy walk with the Eddy man. Jimmy walk with the Eddy man.

Ian comes last and closes the kitchen door behind them.

The three men continue walking together in silence until they reach the pig house. Ian shuffles his feet and looks down most of the time. Jimmy walks on his tiptoes, looking up at Ian from time to time to see if he can see his eyes; but Ian ignores him.

Ian is given his orders, beginning with mucking out the pigs, and then the usual jobs of the day. Ian listens and replies in his usual deferential manner,

'Yes, sir.'

It isn't a heartfelt reply but it sounds humble enough to satisfy Eddy.

And then Eddy turns his head to speak to Jimmy. He reminds him he has a job to do in making a special house for them. Jimmy thinks about the words he has just heard. He heard them earlier that morning but they went away when he was introduced to the Ian man. The Ian man has frightened the words away. But now they are coming back.

Jimmy making a hoose. Jimmy making a hoose.

Then the good song words got bigger.

Jimmy make a hoose for the waron.

He begins to clap louder and louder. He is so happy he dances a big happy hole circle. However, Ian doesn't move. He is making a huge effort to get his thin lips to curve upwards in a 'that's fine with me' smile to disguise how he really feels.

The smile comes but doesn't stay long. Discovering that it will be Jimmy and not him who will be helping Eddy build the Anderson shelter, nettles him. Eddy had promised him the job before he went away. However, he thinks better than protesting about the decision; there are other ways of getting his own back on Jimmy – but it has to be subtle.

Then an idea comes in to his mind. Yes, that will do it; that will really put the cat amongst the pigeons. He smiles to himself as he shuffles away to the barn to begin his work... He is going to enjoy himself after all. There is sweetness in revenge...

Eddy turns to Jimmy.

'Right lad, let's go. I'm your boss now, Jimmy.'

Jimmy doesn't understand the word 'boss' but he likes the sound of the two 'ss' at the end of it. It's like the happy sound the farm cat makes when Snap wants to play chase.

Seven 'to do' purple-song words are now lining up in his head.

Jimmy go with the Eddy boss-man.

Then four more come.

Jimmy make new hoose.

He is excited about what is going to happen next and struts after Eddy towards the shed, where the six corrugated steel panels needed to build the shelter are kept.

Eddy goes in first and Jimmy follows behind him in the same foot spaces that Eddy has taken. The shed is cold but dry. Jimmy likes the shed because the walls are brown like the brown fields he has seen.

Eddy then takes one of the steel panels out of the shed and lays it on the grass.

'Jimmy, can you bring the next one?'

Jimmy understands what is expected of him, so he says, 'Eese.'

It sounds good.

Jimmy do it.

'Well done. Now we will take it in turns to bring all the other four panels out of the shed,' says Eddy.

Jimmy soon gets the idea and both men complete the task with no problems.

'Now we are going to carry the panels up to the farmhouse, one at a time. You take one end and I'll take the other.'

Jimmy know the word 'carry'.

'Like this.' Eddy demonstrates the action he wants Jimmy to make. Jimmy watches it all and feels good about doing it, so he says, 'Eese.'

And it sounds good again.

And the purple happy-song words in his mind tell him he can.

Jimmy can do it.

89

And he does do it and he is pleased when he sees the Eddy boss-man smile.

'Now, Jimmy, there are six panels and I am going to read what we do next,'

He takes out the instruction sheet he has put in his pocket and silently reads.

It all looks simple. All he has to do to make the sides is to bolt the six panels together and one of them will be the door.

Jimmy stands still as Eddy reads the instructions, but his mind is very busy. He is finding it difficult to see how the long, hard things he has carried with the Eddy boss-man can possibly make a hoose. He remembers the hoose he shared with Grandma and it was as big as the sky. He knows this is true because birds sat on it and they flew off it into the bird sky world. He is still puzzling this out when Eddy speaks again.

'Now Jimmy, I want you to hold one of the panels while I fasten it with a special fastener.'

'Eese.'

It still sounds good.

And the purple happy-song words sing again and tell him he can.

Jimmy can do it.

'Well done, now we are going to do that again.'

The action is repeated with the remaining panels. Jimmy does as he is instructed to do. Then suddenly it is done.

It is a hoose and he can stand inside it and it has a roof and a door. He is so happy he begins to jump up and down and he is in the sky and he feels its gentle kiss. It is a kiss like the ones Grandma gave him as a child. Eddy sees the delight on Jimmy's face. He is pleased that all is going well.

'Now, lad, we haven't finished yet. I have to dig a hole and put the house in the hole.'

Jimmy is very excited at the word 'hole' – a hole for the hoose to go in. He is really enjoying himself now and has forgotten all about Ian standing on his foot and his hurting toes.

'Now, you can help me dig the hole. I will get us some spades.'

'EESE.'

This time it is a big sound. And once more the purple happy-song words sing again and tell him he can do it.

Jimmy can do it.

He is now ecstatic. The excitement of it all is filling his head with a happy, fizzy feeling. He has done everything right so far, but above all he knows all about holes and how to make them.

Jimmy know dig.

Jimmy see Eddy boss-man get spades from shed.

'We need to dig the hole about this much,' instructs Eddy.

He then shows Jimmy how deep to dig the hole, and the two men work together side by side until the job is done.

'Now we have to bury the house in the ground.'

Eddy sees the confused look on Jimmy's face, so he moves the shelter slowly to the hole in the hope that he will understand what he means.

Suddenly Jimmy understands what the Eddy boss-man wants him to do. The big purple words sing to him.

JIMMY PUTS HOOSE IN THE HOLE.

JIMMY HAPPY. JIMMY HAPPY. JIMMY HAPPY.

And once more the two men work together side by side until the roof has a thick layer of soil all over it.

'Now, Jimmy, we have to cover the roof to make it look like a grass bank.'

He doesn't understand what that means but he says, 'Eese.' And it makes him feel a lot better.

Eddy then goes to the shed to get the soil and begins to put it on the roof. Jimmy has learnt by now to do the same as the Eddy boss-man, so that's what he does. And then he sees what it is; it is complete and it is amazing. He has made a hoose and a hole and he has been a good boy and the hoose is just the right size for the waron and he feels very happy indeed.

He is so happy that he does a special happy new-hoose dance and shakes the Eddy boss-man's hand up and down three times.

'Hang on, Jimmy, we still have one more thing to do,' chuckles Eddy. 'We need to give the house a bit of turf to make it strong.'

Jimmy does not know the word 'turf' but he says, 'Eese.' And it makes him feel much, much better.

Once more Eddy goes to the shed, finds the turf, comes back and shows Jimmy what to do. The job is completed very quickly, and then it is all done. The Anderson shelter now stands proud and strong, ready to do its safekeeping job.

For the first time in his life, Jimmy has done a man's work and experienced the joy that comes with doing something well. He looks at the new hoose and the sight of it makes him as happy as he was when he first played in the cat water hole.

'Right, then, lad, it's time to eat.'

Eddy then produces a square tin and a flask from his pack-up bag and they eat thick beef-paste sandwiches and drink hot sweet tea.

Everything is getting better and better. Jimmy has eaten wonderful sandwiches and now all he has to do is find Grandma. He feels tired now. It is a happy tired, though, and he knows his toes and his arms want a rest; so he sits down, buries his toes in the grass and pats them gently.

Eddy too is feeling tired. He has been feeling more tired than usual recently and he has been having really bad headaches. They have made him irritable, he knows that.

He hasn't said anything to Mary about the headaches. The thought of illness or worse horrifies him. He thinks about the farm and its future; somehow it has to keep going even with a war on. And maybe Jimmy will become useful; he is certainly strong.

But as for now he has forgotten what he was going to ask Jimmy to do for the rest of the afternoon.

'Jimmy, I'm tired, find Ian and ask him to give you some jobs to do.'

Jimmy hears the new words but he doesn't like them.

Jimmy does not want to find Ian.

Ian hurt Jimmy's toes.

He doesn't move. He doesn't know what to do.

Eddy notices the confused look on his face, and realises what he has said. The lad can't speak clearly, and of course he can't ask Ian what to do.

'Look, I will write it down for you.'

He then takes a pen out of his pocket and the Anderson shelter instruction leaflet and begins to write on the back of it. He then hands it to Jimmy.

'Give Ian this piece of paper.'

Once more Jimmy doesn't know what to do. He wants to do what the Eddy boss-man says, but he doesn't want to find Ian. He wants to look for Grandma. He sits still. However, he takes the piece of paper from the Eddy boss-man's hand because he thinks it is the right thing to do; but still he doesn't move.

'Jimmy, go to that big barn. Ian is there.'

Eddy points in the direction he wants Jimmy to go.

But Jimmy still doesn't move. It is as though his toes are stuck in the ground.

'Do as I tell you.' Eddy's voice has an angry tone in it now.

The loudness of it shocks Jimmy, and Eddy too is startled that he could have sounded so sharp. It makes him jump up and propels him towards where he is told to go. Without wanting to, he finds himself walking towards the barn.

Eddy is now feeling more tired than he has felt in a long time. He has to find somewhere to rest. Then he remembers the old rickety chair that is in the shed. It doesn't take him long to find it. It is a relief to sit down and be out of it all for the time being. His head has 100 hammers in it and he feels dizzy, so very dizzy.

CHAPTER
9

Jimmy has now arrived at the barn.

The Eddy boss-man has told him to go to the barn and he knows he has to do what he is told; but it is not the right time. It is the right time to look for Grandma and his hoose, and the nice Mary-Jimmy lady will make Pease pudding for them all and the Eddy boss-man will be pleased again and the Ian man will be good and everything will be good and he will have happy toes again.

But his toes have stopped and the rest of him has stopped and now his mind is stopping too.

Jimmy eyes going dark.

The sudden unexpected darkness of the barn takes Jimmy by surprise.

It takes a little while for his eyes to get accustomed to the darkness, but when they do he cannot believe what he is seeing. His mind can't think of any words or see any pictures to put a name to any of the objects in front of him. If it could it would say this is a world within a world, with its own smells and shapes.

It would say that the big rough objects in front of him are called haystacks. It would tell him how men have sown and harvested and with farm-hardened backs and sweaty armpits have stored food away for hungry animals. But he knows nothing of this and all he can do is stare.

There is no noise and no Ian man either, and for a few moments he doesn't know what to do. He has to find the Ian man. That's what he has been told to do. He doesn't want to find the Ian man but the Eddy boss-man has told him to do it. Grandma has always told him to do what grown-ups tell him to do. This has always been easy as all the grown-ups he knows have been good to him, but now he feels all wrong. And now a cascade of red words is jamming his head.

Jimmy's head has lots of Eddy boss-man words.

Jimmy's head is too big.

He puts his hand over his ears to stop it all coming; it is coming at him in pictures which he can smell.

Then it all swirls into a tangled mass and explodes uncontrollably in his head. And all of it is making his chest move fast up and down.

And then the big barn begins to move and the top of it wobbles.

Then his whole body wobbles.

JIMMY FALLING DOWN.

Then darkness.

When he comes to, he thinks for a moment he is in his own bed. Then suddenly the earlier pictures and the smells which go with them come back into his mind. And now there are other smells and sensations running over his body.

Three of them are queuing up in turn. The first one is the poo animal smell of the barn. It goes up his nose and makes the food in his tummy come into his mouth. Next there is the feel of the thin covering of earth which he is lying on. The sticking-out bits are jabbing his arms. Then there are his toes which now have pin bits inside them.

And there are no windows around him. It is making him feel lost. He is supposed to find the Ian man. Where is he? He doesn't know. He has to know, he has to be a good boy. And now big red words are shouting in his head.

Jimmy find the Ian man. Jimmy find the Ian man.

And the words get bigger.

JIMMY FIND THE IAN MAN.

He has to find the Ian man, but how? He has no idea; he doesn't know where to start looking. There are so many big things to look behind, and they are different sizes and shapes and some are on top of each other. He knows he has to begin somewhere, but no words are coming into his head to help him. Then suddenly his toes begin to wiggle and he feels a strong urge to run.

Jimmy run. Jimmy run fast.

Jimmy find the Ian man.

Then he is on his feet; but jumping up quickly makes him feel dizzy and he sways slightly. However, he is determined to find the Ian man and be a good boy for Grandma. He begins running, searching, crawling, stalking every light and dark area of the fathomless barn; peering into high corners, standing on tiptoe to scan gaps and crevices and jumping to look behind tall, unsteady stacks. But the Ian man is nowhere to be seen. He has to find him, as loud red words are bellowing in his head.

Jimmy find the Ian man. Jimmy shout for the Ian man.

He doesn't like shouting but he has to. He has to make an effort. So forcing his mouth open very wide to let the sound out, and leaning forward as far as he can go, he breathes out a sound.

'Eeeun.'

The sound is very quiet and it isn't a happy sound. He knows it is too quiet so he tries again.

'Eeeun.'

This time it is better but still not loud enough and it is still a bad sound, but he knows he has to try again. So with one very big breath he breathes out the sound.

'EEEUN.'

This time it is loud, and the sound of his own voice echoing through the earth-smelly straw spaces in the barn makes him jump. He is also beginning to feel strange. The big breathing he has done is making him feel dizzy again. He shuts his eyes tightly to make it all go away. He must sit down to let his head go back into his neck. He strokes his toes to calm himself down, but the red words keep on repeating in his head.

Jimmy body not stop. Jimmy body not stop. Jimmy body not stop.

He must let his body stop. He must close his eyes. He will stroke his toes again. Sleep will come soon...

Jimmy is now sleeping soundly, oblivious of time or anything that is going on. So he doesn't see Ian slink out from behind a haystack near the entrance to the barn, held by a grappling hook ready to be lowered to feed the horses and cows. Only a number of high-up haystack insects see a satisfied lip curl on Ian's face. The same insects scurry away when smoke-infested spit reaches them.

Ian had seen Jimmy coming to the barn when he had gone out to find a rake. He correctly surmised that Eddy had sent Jimmy to be given some more work to do. He half-expected it and so he hid. He had watched Jimmy's search and eventual exhaustion with increasing pleasure. It was very amusing indeed.

Meanwhile, Eddy, who had fallen asleep, is now waking up. His eyes take in the old familiar wood surrounds and for a moment he wonders why he is there. Then the sight of a very large spider crawling up a spade prompts his memory. Yes, of course, he was making the Anderson shelter. Jimmy helped him and then he felt more tired than he had expected to be; and then the headache had come. The blinding headache. But at least it has gone now.

And the Anderson shelter is now built. Has he just thought that? His memory isn't as good as it used to be.

At least the job is done, and if the Jerries come, Mary and the others will be protected. And he has sent Jimmy to do what? Oh yes, he has sent him to Ian. That's fine. Ian will look after him. Best leave him to Ian and go home, maybe do some office work, and whatever else comes to mind.

In the barn, Jimmy is now waking up. This time it doesn't take him long to remember where he is. A picture-memory of himself looking for Ian comes into his head, but the sleep has been good. It means that he doesn't have to look for Ian now as the time for doing jobs is over.

And different words in his mind are now lining up to push the old ones away. And they have a good colour and sound and he knows them well.

LOOK FOR GRANDMA. LOOK FOR GRANDMA.

He feels a rush of peace go through his body. These are the purple-song words he likes the best. If he could explain to another human being about what he knows, he would say that he hasn't found Grandma by digging out the wiggly-thing water. Also, he hasn't found Grandma by jumping down in the duck world sea. So, behind the sea must be at the other side of the duck water.

That's what he has to do next. But first of all he has to find the way out of the barn. This is tricky as the high haystack in front of him is hiding the way he came in. He tries peering down to see if the haystack has any toes which will help it to move out of the way. It hasn't.

However, it has something bigger than toes; it has an interesting spiky space between another haystack. He tries looking through it but it is too dark and he can't see anything.

100

But then something even more interesting happens. A little wiggly thing is dancing its tiny way along the bottom edge of the haystack. He decides to follow it.

Jimmy move with the wiggly thing.

And slowly, with a few stops, the wiggly thing and Jimmy dance their way along the edge of the haystack and then come to the end. And there it is, the entrance to the barn and the deepening sun of the late afternoon is streaming in and Jimmy jumps three happy-purple jumps and then runs outside.

Jimmy happy now. Jimmy happy now. Jimmy happy now.

Now all he has to do is find the duck sea again and the other side. But where is the duck water? He closes his eyes tightly so that the picture-memories and the purple songs will come. But try as he may, they stay away. They are playing the hide-and-seek game and refuse to be found. And now barren-red words are jabbing him.

Jimmy not see pictures.

Jimmy not hear singing.

He sits down on the damp grass and closes his eyes to make the red words go away. Then he opens them again and looks at his toes to make sure they are still there and that's when he sees the wiggly thing again. It is wiggling its way along the grass and it begins to sing to him.

Grandma behind the sea.

He is glad that the wiggly thing can sing. It makes him feel happy. And the song moves with the wiggly thing and dances along in his head. And the words begin to move his toes and his body feels light and the sun is moving too in the same direction as the wiggly thing, so he decides to follow it. And as he walks he takes great care not to stand on the wiggly thing. It has become his friend. It is exciting walking with the wiggly thing. It is taking him to Grandma.

The sun is not so bright now. He must walk fast to stay in the sun. He must follow the wiggly thing. He looks down but it has gone and now the sun is going too. He will not see Grandma in the dark.

He doesn't want the dark to come today but he knows it will come soon; the black sky will join up with the black ground. Then the blackness will fill all the holes up in the ground. He tries thumping the ground and clapping his hands four times in case there are any goblins. Maybe if he sings, the singing will scare the goblins away. He will sing the Hold hackonald ad a arrm song.

Hold hackonald ad a arrm E-I-E-I-O!
And on at arrm he has sum hicks, E-I-E-I-O!
ith a cuk cuk eer and a cuk cuk are
eer a cuk are a cuk
eggywhere a cuk cuk
Hold hackonald ad a arrm E-I-E-I-O.

It makes him feel a bit better. He will sing it again – but the words won't come; the dark has taken them away.

He must walk faster. He must find the behind-the-sea world. He must find it now.

The goblins mustn't come. The goblins might hurt Grandma.

He must run.
He must run fast.
Red words are coming behind him.
Red words are chasing him.
They are getting bigger.
They are in his head.
Cross bad red words are making his eyes wet.

Jimmy not a good boy.

Jimmy not find Grandma.

Cross bad red words are making his face wet.

Jimmy not a good boy.

Jimmy not find Grandma.

BAD BAD JIMMY.

He wants to stop. He wants Grandma to come but his toes won't stop running. They are taking him away from the farm and the Mary-Jimmy lady and the Eddy boss-man and the waron hoose and the nice sandwiches.

Jimmy toes fast fast fast. Jimmy toes fast fast fast.

Jimmy toes fast fast fast. Jimmy toes fast fast fast.

Now they are digging a hole in his head, bruising his mind and pushing out the earlier good words.

Jimmy toes fast fast fast!

He cannot stop, he mustn't be lost. He must find Grandma.

Strange smells he hasn't smelt before and shadows of things he can't put a name to bombard his senses and jumble them up.

Moving night creatures wake up and begin their mysterious routines. Birds stop singing. The heavy sky is getting blacker and blacker. It fills him up with horror and quickens his heartbeat. He is now in a dark, threatening world. Worst of all, he cannot see what is in front of his toes. He cannot see death until it is too late, too late to stop him from tripping up...

Jimmy falling over.

BAD BAD mess squashing on Jimmy. BAD BAD BAD.

Jimmy is now feeling the full horror of a nameless face smearing his own, the face of a dead rabbit. A host of maggots are now enjoying their free evening meal.

The impact of it all is terrifying; an obnoxious blanket of red is now smothering him.

Jimmy nose smells bad stuff. Jimmy's mouth has wet red stuff. BIG BAD SMELL ALL OVER JIMMY.

His face is now covered with blood and guts, but worse of all is the stomach-heaving stench which has gone all the way down his body.

And inside him is a bad sound, coming up from his chest and into his throat, forcing through his mouth and pushing his lips open. Then with no warning it can take no more pressure. It explodes outwards to the air around him.

Ah Ah Ah AH.

The trees and bushes bounce it back, and the sound coils, viper-like, around him, squeezing his breath.

Frightened, night-time animals dart away, squealing as they move. The high-pitched animal noises and everything else that has happened is too much for Jimmy's senses. This time an even louder sound pushes and screams from his mouth. It shoots out and grazes his ear like a stray bullet from a gun. Jimmy, now paralysed with fear, lies motionless on the dead rabbit, alone and lost.

CHAPTER
10

'Are you telling me Jimmy hasn't turned up?'

Eddy and Ian have met up at the farmhouse as they usually do at the end of the day to review the day's work. Eddy is now looking puzzled.

'Yes, boss, not seen him all day.'

'But I sent him to you. Are you sure?'

'Yes, boss,' replies Ian with an innocent stare.

He must keep the pretence up. Jimmy might become too useful and Eddy might prefer him to himself. He must make sure that it is him and not Jimmy who is vital to the farm surviving in the war. At all costs he must avoid being called up. And with the bit of money he has now, who knows, maybe a partnership in the future, then maybe an accident?

A frown begins to deepen on Eddy's forehead.

'Can't understand it; he knows what he is supposed to do.'

Ian is silent. Eddy studies his face for a moment. He has always been able to trust Ian. But today he thinks he has seen something different in Ian's innocent response. And yet there is no reason why Ian should lie. He is imagining things. He isn't himself today.

'So where is he, then?' Eddy's voice sounds rougher than usual.

'Don't know, boss, hope he's alright.'

Eddy is still feeling slightly irritated but also surprised that Jimmy hasn't done what he was told to do. He seemed so obliging and the morning has gone so well.

'Well, there's only one thing for it,' sighs Eddy. 'I'll have to look for him; bit of a nuisance, though. Can't have this happening too often.'

'Yes, boss, I mean no, boss,' replies Ian.

'You get yourself home. See you in the morning.'

A short time later Eddy begins to tell his wife what Ian has said; he leaves nothing out. She listens patiently and shows the same surprise as her husband when she hears about Jimmy supposedly not reporting to Ian. The one difference for Mary is that she has not the same trust in Ian as her husband has. And yet, why would... no, she must be practical. She thinks about what to do next. 'Tell you what,' she says in her usual calm manner. 'If you start and look for Jimmy, I will ring the nurse and see if she can come a bit sooner, because I've just got a feeling we might need her help.'

'What do you mean?'

'Remember the duck pond incident,' Mary replies delicately.

'Yes, but...

'I don't know why, but whenever there has been a spot of bother it has always involved water,' Mary concludes.

'So what are you saying?' asks Eddy abruptly.

Mary notices the irritation in her husband's voice. However, she decides to ignore it.

'Look, this is a guess, but I wonder if he's tried to find the duck pond again,' Mary answers lightly.

'In that case I'll go down that way and leave you to ring the nurse. Hope this is the end of it. I can't be doing with this all the time.'

He is now beginning to feel exhausted, but he has a job to do and that is that.

Five hours later, Eddy turns in for the night. As he listens to the rhythmic sleep noises coming from Mary, his mind goes over the past evening and his search for Jimmy. It has been a wearisome affair.

He recalls the moment he first heard a noise which sounded like a fox mating. He had not taken any notice of it to begin with, then the realisation came that it wasn't a fox this time. He has heard the sound of foxes mating so many times in his life as a farmer, but this time something about the pitch had not been right.

The sound had been his guide. He knows the lay of the land like the back of his hand, and even in the dark recesses of the woodland area it didn't take him long to find Jimmy. But he didn't expect to find him in the desperate state he was in: cold and covered with dead rabbit guts and in a state of paralysed fear.

It took him a great deal of coaxing to get him to stand up, never mind getting him to move. However, he had managed, and fortunately as they were approaching the cottage the district nurse had arrived and took over. That meant he was able to get back to the farmhouse, have a quick wash and a meal which Mary had kept warm in the Aga. Hopefully tomorrow will not be so difficult and he will not be as tired as he has been lately.

Jimmy wakes the next morning with a vague feeling that all is not right. It is not long before the memories of yesterday come back into his mind. They arrive with a jolt and blend with a heavy, sick non-music feeling that comes from his tummy and works itself up to his mouth.

Jimmy head hurt Jimmy tummy hurt Jimmy go to bumwoodhole. NOW NOW NOW!

And that is what he does for the rest of the morning.

Jimmy go to bumwoodhole. NOW NOW NOW!

The nurse seeing the state Jimmy is in calls the doctor. He comes, and after examining Jimmy says that he will be alright in a few days. It is just the result of the bad experience he has suffered.

But it isn't just the rabbit that has upset Jimmy; it is getting lost and not finding the sea world and getting behind it.

These are dark days for Jimmy.

Every day red, accusing words come at him in a soldier-like straight line. And the words begin to move his toes again. And they make him stand up. And they make him march around the room.

FAST FAST FAST

And they always say the same thing:

Jimmy bad boy, not find Grandma.

And then they get bigger.

Jimmy bad boy, not find Grandma.

And bigger still.

JIMMY BAD BOY, NOT FIND GRANDMA.

The words make him take bigger and bigger steps and he cannot stop.

Jimmy toes ache.

Jimmy feet ache.

Jimmy legs ache.

Jimmy bottom ache.

Jimmy tummy ache.

The red words are now filling his tummy up to his neck. He can't eat the nice sandwiches the Mary-Jimmy lady makes for him. He can't eat the nice dinners the Mary-Jimmy gives him.

NO ROOM LEFT IN JIMMY.

The district nurse promises to keep an eye on him and Mary stays with him for much of the time, but he doesn't respond to their comings and goings. It is as if they are not there. Mary is at her wits' end, not knowing what to do. There is nothing for it; she will have to take a chance in asking Eddy. She will ask him tomorrow. She knows he is still annoyed about the rabbit incident, but who else can she talk to...

The next day at breakfast Mary decides to speak to Eddy. It must be now before he gets too busy with the usual farm stuff. She takes a deep breath and speaks. She will keep it brief.

'Eddy, I'm having problems with Jimmy.'

'Oh, not now, for goodness' sake. I've got my own problems to sort out.'

'There's no need to be huffy about it. You're not the only one with problems.'

'Well things are cosy for you. Women get all the luck.'

Mary wipes a tear from her eyes. Eddy decides to ignore it; he has no time for tears today.

'You have no idea, do you? Be nice to everyone, that's you. Try and solve their problems for them and feel good about it afterwards. And everyone says what a nice person Mary Woodhouse is. Well, you solve it, then; sort it yourself.'

And with that Eddy gulps down his tea and leaves the room, slamming the kitchen door behind him. For a few moments Mary feels stunned.

She can count on one hand the number of times Eddy has been cross with her in their married life, and it has usually been over something very silly. But he has never humiliated her. Her eyes mist over, now full of tears. She wipes them away quickly; she is determined not to cry.

Is it just the war, or something else that has upset him? War can do strange things to people sometimes. And then there is Jimmy. Is Eddy turning against him, and at a time when he most needs a friend? Then a face comes into her mind. A gentle, soft, vague face, and she knows immediately what to do. Thank

112

goodness they had been modern and bought a phone. A quick call would be all it takes.

'So, you're having some problems with Jimmy?'

'Yes, Father,' replies Mary

Father Keith has come straightaway after Mary's anxious phone conversation. He is now drinking the obligatory cup of tea in the farmhouse kitchen. Mary tells him the events of the past few days, leaving nothing out. She concludes with a question that sums up her bewilderment.

'Why this preoccupation with water. What's going on in his mind?'

Father Keith listens with the Catholic patience of one who has heard many confessions and problems. But this one is very puzzling; there is Jimmy's behaviour in hospital and the strange behaviour at the pancake race and now, to add to it, the duck pond incident.

Suddenly, something stirs in his mind, a memory of the day Mrs Bailey came to see Jimmy to tell him about what had happened to his grandma. That tipsy over-loquacious sentence she had come out with... if only he could remember what she said... It had annoyed him at the time, but there has been so much to do lately, what with sick people to visit and this horrible war. Plus his usual work.

He knows Mary is waiting for an answer. If only he knew what to say.

'There's something going on,' he answers with more confidence than he feels. 'And I think it's something deep. What does Eddy think?'

'I wish I – well...' replies Mary with a slight catch in her voice.

Father Keith absorbs the catch and wonders.

'I hope this isn't putting a strain on your marriage.'

'No, no, Father,' Mary says hastily. 'Some things with Jimmy are going well. Sometimes he jumps and dances around and looks happy. He also enjoyed helping Eddy build the Anderson shelter.'

'So why is he wandering off like he does? It's almost like he's grieving the death of his grandma sometimes, and other times he has forgotten her.' Father Keith rubs his cheek thoughtfully. 'The big problem is, he can't tell us. Maybe if I have a word with him he might be able to say something or even point to something. Sometimes he tries to talk and other times he doesn't.'

'Maybe it's because of us not getting it right and not giving him time. But then there are days when I think I am getting through to him,' Mary replies with a catch in her voice again.

'Well, I will certainly have a word with him – and what about me having a chat with Eddy too?'

'Yes, alright, but you won't tell him it's me who said anything, will you?'

Father Keith smiles his answer with a sympathetic look.

'Oh, sorry, Father, I forgot. Catholic priests are sworn to secrecy,' Mary replies hastily with a slight blush on her face.

Father Keith smiles once again, drains the last drops of tea from his cup and then stands up.

'Shall we go and see Jimmy now?'

Mary nods in agreement and the two of them walk to the cottage. They say little on the way. When they get there, Jimmy is sitting in the front room with the district nurse who has just arrived.

'Hello, Jimmy. Hello, nurse.'

The nurse replies with a polite, 'Good morning, Father.' But Jimmy looks blank, as though he has forgotten his old friend.

'Jimmy, its Father Keith,' continues the nurse. 'Father Keith has come to see you.'

'Yes, and if you don't mind, nurse, I need to speak to him alone.'

'Of course, Father,' the nurse replies in the same respectful voice she used before. 'Me and Mary can have a cup of tea and a bit of a chat in the kitchen. Would you like a cup of tea Father?'

'No, thank you, nurse. I've just had one at the farm.'

The two ladies go out of the room together and leave Jimmy alone with Father Keith.

'Jimmy, do you remember me?'

Jimmy has remembered. But he doesn't want to speak. He mustn't speak, he mustn't move his mouth; words frightened him too much when he fell on the rabbit.

He didn't like it when his body made a big noise. A big word-noise had come out of his mouth and had made his ears hurt. He didn't like it when the creepy things on the animal-thing crawled into his mouth. He doesn't want his ears to be hurt again. He doesn't want to say any more words. Words are bad. That is it, for all the time there ever will be, he isn't going to talk ever again, not one word or sound – that is it.

'Jimmy, are you happy?'

No reply, then a long silence.

'Jimmy, do you like living here?'

No reply, another long silence.

'Alright, Jimmy,' Father Keith sighs. 'I will come and see you again. Goodbye, Jimmy.'

No reply.

He walks to the kitchen and knocks at the door.

'Come in, Father,' the nurse calls out.

He opens the door and walks in. Mary and the nurse look at him with enquiring eyes. Father Keith sits down.

'He just won't talk and I can't make him. No one can do that.'

'Well, thanks for trying, Father,' replies Mary, sounding more confident than she feels.

He turns to the nurse who is standing respectfully by the kitchen window.

'Maybe it's some sort of medical problem, nurse?'

'Yes, well, maybe. Perhaps if I have a word with the doctor he can pop up and see him.'

'Yes, please do; it might be some sort of depression, and if that's the case, it's definitely a medical matter,' replies Father Keith. 'In the meantime, just make sure he's cared for. Sometimes it's love that's the answer.'

Mary and the nurse both nod their agreement and Father Keith takes leave of them. Yes, love is sometimes the answer, he thinks as he drives away from the farm. It will be a shame if all their efforts are wasted, especially if Jimmy ends up in St Agnes' House. But if he doesn't improve then that could become a reality and Jimmy will live out his days in an institution. What would Grandma have had to say about that?

CHAPTER
11

'What on earth has been going on here?' Eddy exclaims the following morning.

He can't believe his eyes. His carefully constructed Anderson shelter now lies in ruins on the ground! Who could have done such a thing?

He had woken up really early, wondering if the Anderson shelter was secure enough. So he had decided to put a bit more turf on the roof to make absolutely sure it would survive even the worst weather. It would only take a few minutes before breakfast to finish it off, and then he and Ian could start planting potatoes. Jimmy is still not well enough to do anything.

He set out feeling that at least he had done something to protect them against any possible enemy attack, but now he is looking at a scene of destruction and he is angry, very angry. It will take days to sort it out, and even then it might need new panels as they look as though they have been bent. But what is curious is the way the mess looks.

Each heap of turf has been placed at equal distance from the other in a regular circle with one in the middle. Each has roughly the same amount of turf in it and in the middle of each heap is a dent, again in a circular shape, making each heap look like a giant bird's nest. The panels have been placed lengthways between the circles. To Eddy's eyes it now resembles a place where an ancient form of pagan worship could have taken place. Maybe it is some sort of signal to the enemy. Or is it someone playing a game? That is more likely.

Yes, maybe children from the village with nothing better to do. And yet it seems unlikely that children would walk the distance from the village to the farm and then attack the Anderson shelter. After all, they know there is a war on and folk are building shelters for their own safety.

And now it will mean he will have to start all over again. And he has another headache coming on. They are happening too often now.

Then something in his mind begins to emerge: a picture of circles and dancing movements, a snippet of a jumping figure and now a shadow of a face. It is taking over his thoughts and changing them. The face takes on more flesh and becomes recognisable – it is Jimmy's face, he can now see. It is as clear as the messy turf circle in front of him. And throughout the day the face grows, distorting and plaguing him with a fear which rapidly becomes a living entity.

He must talk with Mary this evening at dinner.

Eddy and Mary are talking together at the dinner table. Jimmy has stayed at the cottage for his evening meal and it has provided an opportunity for Eddy to speak to Mary alone. Eddy has explained to Mary what he had seen that morning.

'I can't believe it. Why would he do such a thing?'

118

'For goodness' sake, it's obvious,' replies Eddy in a terse voice. He is convinced it's Jimmy. His head is throbbing and there has to be a reason for it all. He has made a mistake by taking Jimmy on.

'If you think it's Jimmy, you're wrong. It must have been someone else.'

'He's mad, I tell you.'

'No, you've got it wrong. He's not mad, just very sad.'

'And how do you know?' Eddy's voice is becoming louder by the minute.

Mary is quiet at this; she is not sure herself what is wrong with Jimmy, but she is not going allow anyone to say he is mad – not even Eddy.

'He's mad and he's got to go.'

'No I will not be a party to that,' says Mary defiantly. 'But if you think it is him who messed up the Anderson shelter, let's go and ask him.'

What is she saying? She knows he won't talk, but her heckles are rising and she isn't going to give in.

'What do you mean, ask him? He can't – or won't – speak, you stupid woman.'

'Don't you dare call me stupid,' splutters Mary.

'I'll call you what I like,' Eddy rises from his chair. 'And you will do what I say. He's going to Aggies and you are going to take him there. You will ring them tonight. Not me, I've got enough to do.' Eddy's voice has now erupted in a volcanic explosion.

Mary doesn't reply. The air around them is thick with glued blobs of emotion. He waits for her reply. Then after a few nail-biting moments she speaks: 'We must give him time.' Her voice is quiet but firm.

119

'Just like you, isn't it? Always for the underdog.' Eddy's breaths are coming hard, fast and audible. He leans menacingly towards Mary's face. She absorbs his breath; it makes her feel nauseous. Why is he behaving like this? Is it something in his character that has always been there, or is it because of the war? Has the start of a new war unhinged him in some way?

'Eddy, you're frightening me. It's the war. It's what war does to people, it affects them.'

'It's not the war, you stupid cow.' Eddy's voice shoots out and resounds round the kitchen walls. 'If you say that once more I'll flatten you.'

He can take no more. Anger swells and hardens his fist and suddenly, with one sharp, fast movement, he bounds forward and hits Mary hard across the face. The force knocks her sideways off the chair.

Then he storms out of the room leaving Mary on the kitchen floor, bleeding profusely from the top lip. The action is over, but as she lies there she knows she must protect two lives; but how?

She lies for quite a time, not even trying to mop up the small pool of blood. She doesn't feel afraid that he will come back. She knows he will have gone down to the barn. That has always been his bolthole whenever he wants to think about things or when they have had small tiffs.

Then suddenly she knows what she has to do. It will require a phone call early the next morning. She will go to Dover to Aunty Frieda and Uncle Michael. They will take her in. And she will take Jimmy too. She will explain when she gets there.

Eddy is now in a terrible state. The barn offers no comfort to his aching head. What has he done? A minute or two after

120

he hit Mary he came to his senses and is now recoiling from his own violence. Has he really hit his much-loved wife, or has it been some dreadful nightmare, from which he will wake, relieved that it is morning? A fear which has germinated in him is now battering his very soul. He has always been able to think clearly. He has always been in control of himself.

The pain in his head is excruciating. What has he done? Is he ill? Or worse, is he becoming like Jimmy? Yes, that must be it, he is becoming like Jimmy.

The thought fills him with horror.

Then another thought comes in to his mind, worse than all the others. Has he lost the love of his wife? Will she forgive him? It will be a long night.

And so it is for both of them, alone in their separate sleeping areas. But as sure as night turns to day, the morning eventually comes. And with it its heavy-heart expectations.

'Do you know what you are doing, Mary?'

'Yes, Auntie. Oh, I must go. I can hear the train coming. Jimmy is waiting for me outside the phone box. I'll explain all when I see you.'

The phone call to Dover has been easy. All she has to do now is find a quiet carriage.'Come on, Jimmy, follow me... In here, sit next to me...'

They are on the train! They have made it! It is leaving the station!

Last night had been a terrible shock for Mary. In the small hours of approaching dawn there had been doubts about what she had planned to do. The earlier plan to run away and take Jimmy with her had been formed, but then the enormity of it all suddenly frightened her.

Then as the darkness had turned in to dawn she had felt the first fluttering movements of new life in her womb. Finding out she is pregnant has been a wonderful surprise. She had been waiting for the right time to tell Eddy but he had been so cool towards her lately.

Then a beam of sunlight had crept around the edge of her bedroom curtains illuminating her bedroom and also her heart; the new day was bringing a new resolve. She knew that the future of two lives must come first. Nothing is going to harm her unborn baby and the young man whose future is now at stake.

She glances now at Jimmy. He has his eyes closed. Then he begins to snore and she realises he is asleep, so she relaxes in her seat and closes her eyes too...

Jimmy is dreaming and his sleep-mind pictures are showing him some of the things he has done that day. He often dreams about things he has done during the day. His senses store them up, and if they have been happy things his mind relives them like a happy film. When the things he has done during the day have been sad, the dreams are often just swirls of things coming at him which he can't make out. Often the swirls are red.

In the dream he is dreaming now it is today and the Mary-Jimmy lady is in his bedroom. She says his name and tells him to get up. He thinks maybe he is going to the sea to find Grandma, so he obeys her.

Next he walks with the Mary-Jimmy lady to a truck. Then the Mary-Jimmy lady puts a big bag in the truck. Maybe they are going to have big-hole sandwiches again later on for breakfast. He feels good about that too. He is glad his tummy has stopped hurting because he really wants to eat holes again.

Then the truck begins to go and it is good. It is like chasing the cat when the cat runs away.

And then they move down lots of streets he doesn't know and then they stop in a street he doesn't know either and then the Mary-Jimmy lady looks at him and smiles and says: 'Jimmy, we are going on a train.'

He feels really happy. He is excited. He wants to jump up and down in the truck but he thinks his toes might go through the floor, so he doesn't. Then the Mary-Jimmy lady speaks again: 'And, Jimmy, you are going to see some people who live by the sea.'

And that is when the biggest and best purple sea-word song explodes in his head and repeats around his body.

JIMMY GO TO THE SEA.

JIMMY FIND GRANDMA BEHIND THE SEA.

The Mary-Jimmy lady is taking him to the sea, and everything is going to be good and happy again. And he is his own self again and he is going to find Grandma. Then they go up and down lots of streets. Then they get out of the truck. He waves goodbye to it. Maybe it will go home by itself; he hopes it doesn't get lost.

Then the dream begins to fade. The rest of what happened melts into snippets of different things: eating breakfast somewhere, the train coming along the ground, sitting in it and feeling excited and then the wind blowing them away.

Now the dream is over and Jimmy is sleeping a deep, dreamless sleep.

Mary, too, exhausted by the demands of a flight from home, is sleeping peacefully. The train is gathering speed now and moving south, away from the coal mines and the blather and everything that is familiar.

PART TWO

CHAPTER
12

When Jimmy wakes up, he doesn't know at first where he is. Why is he moving? But then very slowly the events of that morning come back to him. He is on a train!

And now his heart begins to beat fast and even faster with the sound of the train in a happy purple train-song.

Jimmy, a train, a train, Jimmy, a train, a train, a train.

And the best bit comes back into his mind with a happy fast jump and clap. He is going to the sea; the Mary-Jimmy lady is taking him! And the purple haunting beginning of his Grandma-song begins to play in his mind.

JIMMY GO TO THE SEA.

JIMMY FIND GRANDMA BEHIND THE SEA.

Then he becomes aware that the train is slowing down. Things around him are changing; where there had been trees and fields there are now tall hoose things. He does not know the name of some of them, but some are hooses like the one he lived in with Grandma. Maybe the sea will be next? He wants to jump up and down but the song won't let him.

Jimmy hush. Jimmy hush. Jimmy sit still. Jimmy sit still.

And then he knows why. The Mary-Jimmy lady is asleep; he must not wake her up.

Jimmy hush. Jimmy hush.

So he watches and waits to see what will happen next. The train is slowing down much more now and is crawling its way along the long line of train track. He watches, fascinated, as it curls around a bend which he can see from out of his window, and for a moment he is worried it might fall over. But it doesn't and the chuff-chuff noise and the smoke stuff are going away. He is sad about the smoke stuff as he likes the way it jumps in the sky.

There are other trains too and they have their own smoke stuff. But now a new world is jumping in his eyes. He is arriving in a place where there are so many trains; more than that, he has never seen so many people in one place. It is going to be hard to see Grandma.

He looks to see if she is there. His eyes drain every detail outside the window but he can't see her. That makes him feel sad for a moment, but then he thinks maybe she will be at the next train world. He knows that trains do that: stop and start. But then suddenly all his disappointment melts away – he has just seen the biggest and best clock that ever was made.

It says twenty-five minutes past ten, but he is unaware of that. It is its roundness which matters. It is perfect and doesn't change if he moves his head. It has a bendy stick on top of it, which is holding it up. And if he bends his head, the clock changes colour. He wonders if the sun does that to all clocks. He wonders too if there is a string tied to it like the kite he once had, and if so, will it fly in the sky? It is the best, most exciting clock he has ever seen.

He wonders if all the people he can see have come to look at the clock too, but they are running away from it. He doesn't know why. He feels sad that they are not looking at the wonderful clock. Some are running towards trains and some are running away from trains to other people who are standing still. Everything is a jumble of legs and arms. Then there are bairns, lots of them, with little bags in their hands.

But the bairns are not happy; they are crying and cuddling to their mars' coats and making them wet. Maybe they want a clock of their own. He remembers toy clocks. He had been given one as a bairn. It had come from a man near his house who had shouted for ragabones.

He notices one of the bairns is cuddling a doll to her face and crying into its hat which has tiny holes in it. He wonders if the holes will push the crying into the doll's head.

He watches, fascinated, as the mothers give them bullets to suck. He likes bullets, they are his favourite sweets. Grandma gives him some as a treat on his birthday. He watches the bairns get on the train and sees their mars begin to cry. He wonders if their mars have toothache. He remembers having toothache once and a man took the tooth out, and worst of all, he didn't give it back to him.

But here the men are not pulling teeth out, they are pushing bags in barrel things which he does not know the name of.

There are other men too and they all look the same. They are dressed in brown trousers and shirts and hats. He thinks maybe it is because they have played in the soil too much and got them dirty. He wonders if they will be told off and sent to bed early. Some of them are cuddling ladies and some of the ladies are crying too. It seems as if lots of people have toothache. He presses his tongue around his own teeth to make sure none of them hurt.

The next thing he notices are the long seats which people are sitting on. He wonders if they will tip up like a see-saw. He thinks maybe all the crying people will feel happy again if they sit at the end of the long see-saw seats and push them up.

Then his eyes wander away from the long seats to the stairs. They seem to go a long way up and then stop. He decides they must be a good place to be if you want to run, as there are lots of people running up and down them.

Then he notices that the train world has a roof on it. His eyes scan the roof. He likes the wiggly lines on it and the way in which it lets in little bits of sun. He wonders if there are any wiggly-water things that live in the wiggly lines. He likes the roof; it looks like a good place to play. Everything is slowing down now and the train-world roof is beginning to stop. Then the train stops altogether, the doors on the train open and Jimmy's carriage door opens too.

Immediately, the strange sights become a barrage of noise. The shock is overpowering. He covers his ears with his hands to make it all go away, but it is no good. The noise is now in the train. It is a bad, red out-of-tune song. His red words have come back. This time they are about what is happening to him now.

Jimmy want NO noise. No noise NO. No noise. No noise.

A man with brown clothes and a loud, thick voice speaks.

'These seats taken?'

A sickening smell of beer descends into the carriage and goes all around the inside of Jimmy's head. The smell shouts a red warning song.

Jimmy want no mens. Wake the Mary-Jimmy lady up.

But it is too late. Mary wakes up with a start. Her hand moves protectively towards Jimmy's arm.

The brown clothes man doesn't wait for an answer and he and three of his mates pile in to the carriage. To Jimmy their communal brownness makes them look like misshaped mountains.

Jimmy gapes at them with an emotion he cannot name. It isn't exactly fear. It is more like unease. He cannot make them out.

Six people now sit in the train carriage: Mary, Jimmy and four soldiers. The train begins to move again and soon the busy city is replaced with fields, trees and countryside. The previously almost-empty luggage racks are now bulging with army bags. And now six pairs of eyes are trying their best not to stare across the carriage at each other.

Mary stares at a faded bit of blue cloth on the armrest of one of the seats opposite. She still feels uneasy and is silently hoping the soldiers will get off at the next stop.

The soldier sitting opposite Mary is now gazing at a photograph which he has taken out of his pocket. He is absorbing the clear, cheeky spirit in the eyes of his sweetheart. The beer hasn't helped with their parting.

131

The one sitting next to him is idly fidgeting with a button on his jacket which his wife had sewn back on before he left home. It is the last thing she touched before kissing him goodbye. The beer hasn't helped him either.

The third soldier, who is older than the others, is the one who is feeling the most embarrassed. He is feeling old and tired. The early signs of wrinkles have aged him more than his years and hide the fact that he is still young enough to go to war. He looks at the door and idly muses that he has gone through too many wrong doors in his life.

The fourth soldier, the one who had come in to the carriage first, wears a frown in his eyes but holds his head high in a defiant stare. He sniffs occasionally. The war has interrupted his plans. He has no time for killing, although he is no coward. He had plans to rise up in the retail business. He is young with no ties. This isn't how he wanted it to be.

Jimmy wonders if the brown clothes sniff man has something stuck in his nose. He once put a marble up his nose to see how it felt. Grandma had managed to fish it out with a knitting needle. Then his nose had started to bleed. He had hidden the knitting needle under Grandma's bed. Grandma had found it after lots of days and she had clouted him on the head.

He wonders too if the brown clothes man who is playing with his jacket button likes holes. Buttons are like holes, a good round shape.

He then wonders if the brown clothes man who is looking at the bit of paper in his hand is praying. He has held bits of paper in church when the people talked together.

Then he turns his head to look at the brown clothes man who is looking at the door. Perhaps there is something behind it. He wonders if the man likes to play the hide-and-seek game. Lastly, he looks again at the brown clothes sniff man who said the three bad words and woke the Mary-Jimmy lady. He wonders if his nose is alreet now but he is now looking at the wall. Jimmy wonders if the man wants to cuddle the walls like he did at the cottage. But the brown clothes sniff man doesn't move so Jimmy thinks maybe he has gone to sleep with his eyes open. He looks at him for a long time, waiting for him to wake up. It is a mistake, for suddenly he turns his head to speak to the soldier sitting next to him and catches Jimmy staring at him.

'What yer starin at?'

Jimmy is aware he is being spoken to but he doesn't know what to do. He simply keeps on staring.

Mary stays silent. She is tired, so very tired. She wonders if the shock from being hit is now taking its toll. She glances nervously at Jimmy but can't tell by the impassive look on his face what he is thinking. However, she is worried about what he might do. Supposing he did something unexpected, like he did at the duck pond? Should she get up and find another compartment? She begins to stand up. However, her hopes are dashed by another soldier opening her carriage door in the hope of finding a seat. Finding every seat full, he grumbles some remark about being no spare seats in the entire train. Mary and Jimmy are now stuck and feeling very uncomfortable indeed.

The sniff soldier is now in his element. He decides to focus his attention on Mary.

'So who is he, then, your boyfriend?'

'Shut up, Ken.' The older soldier remonstrates again. He is now feeling very annoyed with his mate. The other two soldiers

133

are feeling the same but lack the confidence to speak up. Their beer courage has worn off and now they are just two scared raw recruits going off to war.

There is an uncomfortable silence and Mary feels its full impact. She sits very still with her back fully erect against the train seat.

'Cat got your tongue as well, love?'

The words are hardly out before Jimmy's body reacts violently. The sight, smell and sensation of creepy-crawly things from the dead rabbit on his tongue have left an indelible mark in his memory. And now the thought that the same thing could happen to the Mary-Jimmy lady revolts him.

And then a new sensation hits his body with an emotion he has not felt before in his life. The part of his body he has always liked the best is his feet and especially his toes. But now he is suddenly aware of his hands in a new, startling, but exciting way. They are screwing together into a tight ball and his arms feel stronger too. It is a special feeling and a very new one.

He lifts his screwed hands up to his eyes and to his surprise he notices his fingers have gone white. It is the whiteness of anger, the anger of an emerging man.

It has begun, the beginning of the child becoming a man; the chrysalis stage of what is yet to come has started. He has also been observed.

'Want a fight then do yer, big boy?' demands the sniff soldier.

'No, he doesn't.' Mary's quick reply defrosts her taut body. She has had enough.

'Come on, Jimmy.' And with that final statement she grabs their luggage and Jimmy's arm and, ignoring the sardonic laughter of the soldier pushes her way past four pairs of knees and out into the waiting corridor. Jimmy, too surprised to do anything or even to try to speak, follows her meekly, his hands and arms relaxing back to how they had been before the fracas started.

Mary breathes a sigh of relief to be in the relatively fresh air in the corridor. However, her mind is now reeling with the shock of the soldier's cutting words. They have gone deep. Is that how it looks to people, her and Jimmy together, a couple? Then a new, horrifying thought slices into her brain, making her wince. Is that what they will be thinking at home, that she has run away with Jimmy? And of course they, as well as Eddy, will have no idea she is pregnant. Her reputation is now in question; could she ever go back?

She has left her husband and is now journeying into the unknown; a sudden panic seizes her heart. She notices that the train is slowing down and approaching the next station. Should she get off and go back home? No! Once more her heart shouts no, she cannot, the risk is too great. She takes a deep breath. She feels so very tired and the noise around her is making her feel sick. She knows she has to get to the toilet even though the train will stop soon. Her body is now heaving with nausea. The compelling impulse that she has to eject the contents of her stomach cannot be ignored, but is it safe to leave Jimmy by himself? She must, she has no choice. Her throat is taut with vomit.

'Jimmy, I am going to the lavatory. You must stay here.' She inwardly congratulates herself on sounding calm, but there is no time to lose. She flees to the nearest toilet and hurriedly locks the door.

Jimmy is left standing by the train door. He thinks the Mary-Jimmy lady has said something but he hasn't heard every word. The only word he has clearly heard is the last one, 'here'.

The train is slowing down even more now. Jimmy notices he is coming in to a different train-sleeping place with a different roof and a different clock. Then with one enthusiastic steam gush, it stops. This must be it. He is here. He is here! The sea must be here. Grandma must be here. The hoose must be here too. It has come from the farm and Grandma is here with the waron.

The men in dirty clothes are opening the door. He must look for Grandma. The familiar Grandma-song starts once more in his head:

JIMMY GO TO THE SEA. JIMMY FIND GRANDMA.

And it is filling his head and every space of his body. The happy purple song is urging him onwards.

JIMMY GO TO THE SEA. JIMMY FIND GRANDMA.

The dirty clothes mans are getting off the train. He must follow them. One happy jump step and he is off too. He must walk quickly. He must find the sea. It only takes a second for a war swarm of people who are now crowding the platform to swallow him up.

Mary comes out of the toilet feeling much better both in her mind as well as her body. It is as though she has sicked up all the stuff she has been thinking as well as the contents of her stomach. Her reputation now seems insignificant compared to the safety of her unborn child and Jimmy. She wonders how she could have ever thought such things.

She looks around for Jimmy. Where is he? Has he gone to the toilet too? A lot of people are getting off the train now, most of them soldiers. It is taking a lot of time and the platform is filling up with people. Adrenalin is now rising from her empty stomach and for a moment distorts her vision; and then panic takes over. Where is he? Has he followed the soldiers? Does he think she has got off? She has been a while in the toilet but that couldn't have been helped.

She pushes her way to the corridor door, ignoring protests from people who are getting off the train, and steps onto the platform. Her eyes scan the scene in front of her but it is difficult to see over a multitude of heads. She stands on her toes and strains her neck forward. That is when she sees him and to her horror he is walking towards the steps that lead out of the station.

'Stop, Jimmy! Jimmy, stop!' she hollers.

But there is no response. What can she do? The train will be going soon. Suddenly she spots a porter very close to where Jimmy is walking.

'Stop him!' she yells, but the noise on the platform drowns her voice.

'Who do you want, my dear?'

A voice behind her makes her jump. She turns around to see who is speaking. A well-dressed man, whom she guesses is in his early sixties, is looking kindly at her. He has the air of a onetime military man.

'It's Jimmy tell him – tell him.' Mary blushes at her own attempts to speak normally.

'Now, just relax, tell me once more.'

She pauses and tries again.

'Tell that porter to bring Jimmy back,' she begs. 'Please, he has to come back.'

The stranger takes command immediately.

'Hey, you man, porter!' he bellows. 'Get that lad next to you and bring him here.'

Heads turn at the sound of the stranger's command as it bolts down the platform. Some think the escapee is a deserter. So does the porter. He is a big man and likes his job, although his dour face doesn't show it; it has earned him the nickname Smiley from his workmates.

This is a voice he must obey. He has to do his bit for the war effort. No one gets away from Smiley. He springs towards Jimmy and grabs him by the arm.

'Now then, lad, where do you think you're going?'

The shock to Jimmy is profound and immediately big red words overtake his mind.

Jimmy sees man's arm on Jimmy's arm.

He tries to struggle, but the porter is too strong for him. He tries again but it is no use. He is being unceremoniously frogmarched back to the train. He has to find Grandma and he is being prevented from doing so. He wants to cry out but his mouth remains tightly closed. He tries one more wriggle, but the porter's arm is too strong. He has carried too many cases to worry about a struggling youth.

'You come with me. They're waiting for you, lad, on the train. You're going to the seaside!' The porter laughs at his own sarcasm.

Jimmy only understands the last word of the porter's sentence, but it enters his head like a shot from a gun. Then Mary speaks.

'Not here, Jimmy, it's the wrong here.'

The wrong here?

'Get back on the train Jimmy. It's the wrong here. It's beginning to go.'

She makes a quick dash for the train followed by the stranger.

The wrong sea?

Jimmy get back on the train.

They are running now, the porter and Jimmy; both men are running alongside the train and it is gathering speed. It looks as if they are not going to make it. Suddenly the stranger with the sergeant major's voice has an idea. Grabbing hold of a bag, which has been shoved behind the train door, he throws it out on to the platform.

'Jimmy, grab hold of this'

Jimmy cannot get the bag.

'He can't reach,' pleads Mary.
'Come on, lad, you can do it.'

Jimmy can do it.

'Grab the strap, lad.'

With one huge leap Jimmy grabs hold of it, and the old man, with the strength of Hercules, hauls him in. It has been a close thing. Jimmy now lies sprawled out on the floor of the train, puffing and panting. His breaths are coming short and fast, but at least he is safe.

'Thank you, porter!' shouts Mary as the train moves away.

For a moment a damp smile drips from the porter's lips and moistens his face. Then it returns to its normal parched expression. He stands still for a few minutes, recovering from the exertion of it all, and then moves off, feeling very pleased with himself.

The stranger has moved away to allow Jimmy to sit down, and is now looking out of the corridor window. Mary walks the few steps to where he is standing.

'And thank you too,' she says with a warm smile.

'It was luck, that's all,' he replies. But his wide-faced grin shows he is pleased with his herculean efforts.

Mary smiles her thanks once more and then turns towards Jimmy who is now sitting up on the train floor, with his back to the corridor wall. He is still panting. Thinking it will help him if she sits down next to him, she does so. Together they sit side by side in the corridor next to their bags, ignoring the strange looks of people passing by. They sit for a while until she feels that Jimmy is better. Then, choosing her moment carefully, she speaks.

'Jimmy, we need to find somewhere to sit.'

Jimmy stands up and silently they set off to find a new carriage. Fortunately, a large number of people had got off at the previous station, leaving spaces in a number of carriages.

Eventually they find a carriage which to Mary looks safe – it only has one person in it, an elderly lady. She has been reading but has closed her book.

'Excuse me, but is the carriage free?' asks Mary.

'Yes, dear.'

'Thank you.' The relief in Mary's voice is audible.

Mary settles into her seat with Jimmy next to her, and closes her eyes.

But Jimmy has his eyes wide open. He has to; he is getting nearer to finding Grandma, and the train is singing his song.

JIMMY FIND GRANDMA doesdly dum doesdly dum doesdly dum doesdly dum. Sing with Grandma doesdly dum doesdly dum.

It will stop at each station and then continue when the train moves again.

JIMMY FIND GRANDMA doesdly dum doesdly dum doesdly dum doesdly dum. Sing with Grandma doesdly dum doesdly dum.

And on it goes and the song climbs to a crescendo, and every passing tree chucks it along and echoes it forward to its destination.

CHAPTER
13

He is here. Mary has told him it is the right here. The train put them down in a big train home which had lots of running people which made him feel dizzy, but then he saw the biggest clock he had ever seen and it was the best hole ever. Then he got on another train which had lots of brown men too. They sang laughing songs and patted him on the head. He was glad the men had liked his head. He had eaten lots of good hole sandwiches and drunk lots of tea. Then he got off the train at another train home and a car had taken him to some new people. Now he is hoping the new people will help him find the sea and Grandma. Now he is very happy. He will jump three happy jumps.

Jimmy jumping in the air.

Jimmy come to a shop.

A shop with a hoose on top.

Hoose in the sky.

Jimmy wonders if the people in it walk in the sky. That will be like jumping in holes that have no bottom.

It is a hoose in a town he has never been to before with a name he doesn't know, but that doesn't matter; it is the right here.

He goes inside with the Mary-Jimmy lady.

But now he is tired. He must go the bed. It is a good tired.

Jimmy does tired open mouth.

The new people are smiling. The new people are showing him where to sleep.

Jimmy lie down.

Jimmy go to sleep.

Jimmy wakes up. He looks around him. Jimmy knows it.

Jimmy come to sea place.

Jimmy come to a shop.

A shop with a hoose on top.

Hoose in the sky.

He has come to a good place and met two new people. He hopes the two new people will give him good sandwiches like the Mary-Jimmy lady did. Very soon he will put his big arms around Grandma's waist and they will sing happy songs and eat bread and marg together. He is so excited that a purple song sings all around his head in a happy circle. The last line is the best one of them all and it sings twice to him:

Jimmy happy.

GO TO THE SEA GO TO THE SEA.

Find Grandma behind the sea.

Find Grandma behind the sea.

Jimmy now feels safe; the two new people have shown him where to eat his dinner and they are now sitting at the table with him. They are smiling at him and talking words he doesn't understand. His eyes look at their mouths and then at their eyes. They are good eyes. They are brown and green and a bit wet. He wonders if the good people like cat holes like he does.

He is glad that Mary is sitting next to him. Now his eyes travel to the new man, he is Michael. He is sitting next to Mary.

Sixty-one-year-old Michael Kidd didn't want to follow his dad down the coal mines of Northumberland, so he ran away from home and changed his name. He was lucky to find casual work as a farm labourer on a number of farms. But for fear of being found, he travelled further and further south, and had eventually reached Dover.

He managed to find work at the docks and a short time afterwards he met Frieda. They married a year later. They were lucky; she was left some money from an uncle who died. With it they bought a small grocers' shop in town. Michael has been very happy to run it, and soon both of them were working hard to build up a modest but successful business.

Michael has always loved his allotment, as well as messing about with boats with his friend, George. As George owns his own small fishing boat, he is glad of Michael's help with the upkeep of it. Both activities have been an escape from home for Michael when he is weary from running the shop.

Jimmy's eyes now look at Frieda, who is sitting next to Michael. Frieda, although not a gossip, knows how to talk well and can relate to anyone. Her work in a nursing home has brought her into contact with a variety of vulnerable and lonely people. She has befriended many a waif and stray. Together Michael and Frieda have brought three sons in to the world, two of whom were twins. The twins had enlisted during the last year of the Great War; they weren't eighteen but had wanted to 'get out there' and so had lied about their age. Their parents had strongly disapproved of this, especially Frieda, who has very strong opinions about the way in which the 'big uns' in power were running things. Sadly, both were killed in action. Their youngest son, Todd, distinguished himself by going to university and becoming a solicitor. London with its promise of success has claimed him for its own.

Jimmy is now feeling very happy indeed.

He likes the food he is going to eat. There is stew and dumplings on his plate. He looks at everyone's plate. They have the same food as him. It is a good meal. He will eat the food and it will fill his toes. His toes will be strong. He will be able to look for Grandma tomorrow.

The following day finds Jimmy standing in the grocers' shop. He has been told to go there by the Mary-Jimmy lady, who is now with him. Mary has decided that Jimmy needs to see the shop. He may be able to help Uncle Michael. Jimmy had wanted to start to look for Grandma, but it is raining very heavily and Grandma always told him to stay indoors when it rains. But indoors has never been like this.

He has never been in a shop that has so much food, and it is all crowded together on shelves. At least, that's how it looks to him. Tins, bottles, packets and jars with names that he can't read are now flooding his mind. Their colours are cascading together in a food waterfall.

But best of all there is jam.

A very enormous, happy-purple food-song buzzes in his brain.

Jimmy sees lots of good eaty things. Jimmy likes it all.

Jimmy is lost in his happy food song. It sings from every corner of the shop and makes him jump three times with happiness.

He is just about to peer closer at the jam when a sudden noise behind him makes him start. He twists around to see who it is. A lady he doesn't know has just entered the shop. She trips up and almost loses her balance.

'Whoops, should av picked me feet up! I'm Meg, it rhymes with peg! It's my birthday next month. Ize be twenty-four. You're Mary, ain't you? I've seen yer photo, I've seen yer on the mantelpiece!'

Meg Moss is one of Frieda's waif and strays. Meg had so appealed to Frieda's caring nature that Frieda had persuaded Michael to take her on as an assistant in the shop. Michael agreed not so much as to please Frieda but because it would give him more time to do the shop finances, which becoming more difficult as he gets older. Meg has now become like one of the family. Her chief delight is being invited to Sunday dinner.

She darts across the room towards Mary to look at her more closely.

147

'You, it's you on the mantelpiece, next to the blue vase,' she concludes with a nod of triumph.

'Yes, hello, Meg, nice to meet you, and this is Jimmy,' replies Mary in her best polite voice which has successfully swallowed a laugh.

Jimmy stares at Meg incredulously. He wonders why the Mary-Jimmy lady would want to be on the mantelpiece next to the blue vase. Maybe it is to keep warm by the fire, he thinks.

Jimmy cannot stop staring at Meg. He has never seen anyone so thin and with such a lot of hair. He likes the hair. It reminds him of the very tall grass he had seen by the wiggly-thing water, all thick and jumbled up. He looks at Meg's eyes and likes them too. They are big and open and have a smile in them. They are good eyes. His purple words tell him what to do next.

Jimmy shake hands with the Meg lady.

Jimmy shake hands three times.

So he does.

Meg complies with the unusual greeting as she still feels a bit silly about her clumsy entry to the shop a few minutes earlier. Above all, she wants to be accepted by this new male stranger. It is exciting to have a young man shake her hand. She speaks again, her words tumbling over each other,

'Don't mind me, Jimmy. Mother sed Iz was born with too many arms and legs! Iz born all mixed up. That's what Mother sed.'

Mary is quick to squash any self-degradation.

'Now, that's not true. Uncle Michael's told me all about you. He says you're a treasure.'

Meg doesn't ask for explanations of why Mary is there or even who Jimmy is. Her mother has always said don't ask too many questions. However, an obsessive nervousness about what Mary might know about her background suddenly fills her head with alarm. She has to ask just one question and then she will stop.

'Do you know about me, Mary?'

'A little bit,' replies Mary.

'Mother says it's my fault, yer know.'

Mary has no idea of what Meg may have done to annoy her mother, but thinks it is wise not to pry.

'Mother says it's my fault, yer know,' she repeats, and then closes her eyes in an effort to block out the hurt. A slight pause follows as Mary chooses to continue her silence.

'Mary, Iz a workhouse kid and Mary, it's bad, very bad. Iz one kid too many and Mother can't look after us, specially after Father scarpered. There ain't no money and then one day she goes away for a bit and then she comes back and then they puts us in the workhouse. Iz tries to run off but they catched me and brought me back. Iz got out at eighteen when it shut and then Iz met Frieda. Iz has my own place now.'

Jimmy, who has been listening to all this, is now looking very distressed. He hasn't understood most of the words Meg has been saying, but he understands the words 'bad, very bad'. He doesn't want to hear any more about 'bad, very bad', so he puts his hands over his ears.

Meg sees him and immediately panics.

'Jimmy, Iz alright. Why is he doing that? Tell him, Mary, Iz alright.'

'It's alright, Jimmy. Why don't you shake hands with Meg again?' Mary feels she is clutching at straws but she can't think of any other way to help the suffering Jimmy.

Jimmy hears the words 'shake hands' and immediately the bad words go away and he feels better.

Good words from the Mary-Jimmy lady.

Shake hands, Jimmy, shake hands.

But he is curious about the Meg lady's arms and legs. He needs to know if she has any more that he cannot see. So as he shakes hands with Meg for the second time; he moves his arm to the right to shake it. Meg has to move her arm to match his. A tangle of two arms is the result but it gives Jimmy the chance to see if Meg has any more arms.

He is surprised to see there are no more arms. And at close range he can also see that the Meg lady has the right number of legs. He wonders about this; maybe the Meg lady has lost the others and if so has her mother been cross with her. Grandma was once cross with him when he took a leg off her rocking chair. He wanted to see if the leg would rock by itself. He was disappointed when it didn't move.

Meg has no problems with being scrutinised. She knew all sorts of people in the workhouse. If they did strange things, well, it was just the way they were, and after all, doesn't she have movie star eyes? To her they are the same colour and shape as Dorothy Lamour's, deep dark-hazel with well-formed eyebrows. No one minds that Meg 'romances' a great deal; it is her way of covering up her soul-gashed wounds of the workhouse.

Jimmy is now very happy. He likes all the new people he has seen.

The rest of the day holds no more surprises for Jimmy and goes by in one big time jump. There had been other peoples in the shop and lots of plates of food which had filled his toes. And he had felt safe when the big dark came.

And now, coming to the end of the day, it can be allowed to depart with nothing more to commend it.

CHAPTER
14

'What do you think about all this?'

It is Sunday morning and Michael and Frieda are enjoying a lie-in with their usual cup of tea.

'Mary or Jimmy?'

'Both,' replies Michael in his usual succinct way.

'Right then, Mary first. Basically, she's scared to death about Eddy finding her, but and I know for a fact she still loves him. 'Alright, but what do we do?'

'Do you think he will try and contact her here?' Frieda asks.

'Well, yes, I suppose so,' replies Michael.

'But we mustn't interfere; we have just got to let her sort it out for herself.'

'Well, yes suppose so' repeats Michael. He is really at a loss with matters of the heart. 'And Jimmy?' he continues.

'Mary hasn't told me a lot about him yet, except something about his safety. Reckon she'll tell me in her own time.' Frieda pauses to drink a mouthful of tea. She continues speaking. 'Apparently Jimmy had a nurse back home to look after him, and she got him to do a few things for himself.'

'Do you mean going to the toilet and all that.'

'He's fine with the toilet, but it's shaving he hadn't got the hang of. Mary says the grandma babied him a bit. But he can do it now. We'll manage with the rest of it. This morning is was a decent start; he's gone off to church with Mary and Meg.'

Michael goes quiet for a few moments. He feels a little uneasy about it all. Then he speaks: 'It's a bit unusual having him here. We don't really know him.'

'Look, my love, there's a war on, and who knows what might happen to any of us. He can help you in the shop, what with your back and you not getting any younger.'

Well, that's true, but...'

'Let's just take one day at a time.' It is Frieda's last word and she has that note of persuasion in it that he knows so well.

The morning goes by slowly for Michael. He spends most of the time up to dinner reading the newspaper. He knows Meg has been invited to Sunday lunch. Sunday lunch, in their abode, is a traditional roast dinner; always delicious with plenty of gravy. He likes lots of gravy, especially on his Yorkshire puddings. Frieda is still making them, despite the war; he hopes there won't mean any more rationing.

Dinner comes eventually, and Frieda's gravy is up to her usual standards. After dinner, Meg looks at Jimmy in the hope that he will smile at her. Smiling could be he likes her a lot. Jimmy, however, is looking out of the window. He has just seen two birds fly together across the sky. He is wondering if they are looking for their hoose. Frieda and Michael are hoping that their Sunday afternoon nap won't be scuppered. Mary had noticed the furtive looks which had passed between them shortly after dinner finished. She says she will wash up and suggests a walk to Meg and Jimmy.

She finishes the sentence by saying: 'You might have time to see the sea.'

Huge purple-song words bounce into Jimmy's head. At last he is going to see the sea! He will find out what the sea looks like! He will find Grandma and everything will be right again!

GO TO THE SEA GO TO THE SEA.

Find Grandma behind the sea.

He jumps three happy jumps.

'Jimmy, the sea's good,' Meg replies eagerly.

At last the time has come when she can be alone with Jimmy. Perhaps he will hold her hand? She hurries off to get her coat and then waits for Jimmy to get his. He takes his time. He must fasten all the buttons on his coat from his legs upwards. He must keep his legs warm so that his toes will be warm too and then they will work well. His toes must work well. They will take him to find Grandma.

'Jimmy, yer ready, then?' Meg hollers out.

He wants to shout out yes in a big-boy voice, but his tongue sticks to the roof of his mouth. Instead he bounds up to her in three happy jumps.

'Don't yer speak, then?'

Meg's direct question-words sting his brain. He wants so badly to speak; especially as the last few happy days have taken the bad memories away. And now words are coming into his mouth; but it has been so long since he has tried to talk that he has no idea what to do with them. He opens his mouth and tries breathing them out, but at each attempt all he can make are feeble breath echoes.

Jimmy's strange sounds startle Meg and she turns to look him full in the face. She is alarmed to see Jimmy's mouth still twitching with the effort of it all. Immediately she knows that he badly wants to speak. An empathy gained by so many years in the workhouse has made her very sensitive.

'Jimmy, Iz sorry, Iz very sorry.'

And in the same instant Jimmy knows he has found a friend. It is going to be a good walk day. Meg shouts out 'tarrah' and together they walk to the front door and outside to begin their walk

Meg is wisely silent.

Jimmy has never seen so many streets; some wide, some narrow, all of them Sabbath-quiet. Only a few late-April walkers are out and about, some of them with hunched bodies mirroring the vigour of a strong sea breeze. Jimmy loves the force of the wind. It has its own strong purple-song which swells his face and makes it tingle.

Jimmy feel big.

Jimmy feel big big.

Jimmy feel big big big.

And it moves him along happily, blissfully, and with the joy of movement that now belongs only to the wind and Jimmy together. Meg, however, is not enjoying the wind and is more concerned for Jimmy's safety. The main problem is that Jimmy keeps on straying to the side of the road; whether this is the wind or excitement, well, who knows. And he is not holding her hand. There is nothing for it; she will have to do the asking.

'Jimmy, is yer going to hold my hand?'

Jimmy hear Meg lady's words.

But they make no sense. Why should he hold the Meg lady's hand? He just can't think of a reason that makes sense. Fortunately, he doesn't have to, for suddenly a voice speaks from behind them.

'Hello, Meg.'

Meg turns around. She recognises the voice as belonging to a lady customer who comes into the shop at least twice a week. It is the Polish lady with the name she can't say because it has too many difficult letters, out walking with her dog. Meg grins; she loves dogs.

'Oh, it's Rusty! Is yer alright, Rusty?'

Rusty's owner laughs at Meg's concern about Rusty's health over her own. She doesn't mind, though, as she has always liked Meg.

'He's fine. Who is this you have with you?'

'Oh, he's Jimmy,' replies Meg, in a matter-of-fact way.

'He seems keen to be off.'

And yes, Jimmy is keen to be off. Any interruption, whether red or purple, isn't going to distract him from getting to the sea and finding Grandma. Meg speaks again to Rusty, who rewards her with a doggy tail-wag.

'Well, I won't stop you here; must get back to the old man. He'll be walking Rusty himself soon. It's a pneumonia he has got but as you English say he is out of the woods now.'

The effect on Jimmy is immediate. Ugly, misshapen red words shoot into his brain, bringing back a memory he thought had gone away.

Jimmy in the wood. Jimmy falling over.

Then more red words:

Mess squashing on Jimmy.

Then some more red words arrive, tumbling over themselves, vying to be remembered:

Jimmy nose bad stuff. Jimmy's mouth wet red stuff.

The effect on Jimmy is immediate. He turns in his tracks and, without any warning to Meg, sprints down the road with the speed of an athlete.

'Jimmy, where yer going? Jimmy, come back!' she shouts, charging after him.

Meg's urgent plea makes no difference to Jimmy. His one simple goal is to get as far away from the wiggly eat things as possible, and the red words are still very loud and very red. And they are all coming in one mad rush and in one blood-soaked memory:

Jimmy in the wood. Jimmy falling over. Mess squashing on Jimmy.

Jimmy's mouth wet red stuff.

But then the red words begin to slide down his brain. This has never happened before. They are being powerfully shoved out by a number of very powerful purple-words and a hint of music is beginning. For a moment, the red words fight back, but it is no use; the battle has been lost – the music was the stronger force right from the start. Then the first notes of a gentle song sing in his head. They group themselves together and surround the word 'grand'. The next ones collect themselves around the word 'ma', the next ones blend the word 'behind' within its tune; and then the music quickens and the rest of the song-sentence comes in one crescendo: 'the sea'. With each note the red words die, one at a time, and then the rest collapse in a silent, dead heap. Then they are gone and only the sweet purple music remains. Now all he can hear is:

Grandma behind the sea.

His brain is full of the most exquisite rhythm he has ever heard. Its calming melody is lowing him down until, eventually, he stops running and stands still, giving Meg the chance to catch him up.

'Jimmy, Jimmy, what does yer do that for? You've gotta tell me, you've gotta talk.'

Jimmy, although now calm, is feeling exhausted, so he sits down on the pavement. It seems the most sensible thing to do. Meg sits down too, despite feeling silly. It is Jimmy she is most concerned about. Fortunately, there are only a few people in the street. One or two glance across and simply surmise that they have had too much to drink. They continue walking, not wanting to get involved. After all, the country is at war; a bit of booze blots it all out.

Jimmy has no intention of getting up. He is still panting and trying to get his breath, but the music has been so beautiful that he really wants to tell the Meg lady all about it. He has begun to trust her. This time he won't let anything stop him from speaking.

Happily the words 'Grandma behind the sea' come into his mouth one at a time; it is as though someone is helping him; all he has to do is let them out. He turns his head towards Meg, and in one big breath deliberately breathes the words out to her.

'Anma ehind er ee.'

For Jimmy, that is an achievement: he has talked again and the wiggly things haven't come. However, Meg hasn't understood a word of it. Worst of all, Jimmy knows she hasn't understood him. It is the face look he knows so well. But he mustn't give up. He must tell the Meg lady where Grandma is. He will try again.

'Anma ehind er ee.'

But it sounds the same as before.

Meg still hasn't understood. She knows she has to help, but how can she get Jimmy to talk right? She has to help. That's what she had to do for all the people in the workhouse. She thinks for a while then suddenly a picture of Dorothy Lamour singing comes in to her head. That's it, sing!

'Jimmy, yer knows the im we sings at church this morning? The one about morning is broken.'

'Jimmy, sing it.'

Jimmy hear word sing. Jimmy like sing.

He does remember it and immediately a smile comes on to his face. Meg sees the smile and takes it as permission to carry on speaking.

160

'Jimmy, can yer sing yer words to the tune of that im?'

He thinks hard about this. However, Meg doesn't wait for an answer. She stands up and begins to sing the first line to the hymn to prompt his memory.

Morning is broken!
Liker new morning!
Blackburd has spokes on!
Like the first bird.

Jimmy's smile broadens, as he knows the words are not quite right. But will he be able to sing? To be able to sing he has to see if the kind smile is still in the Meg lady's eyes. He gets up and leans forward and stands on his toes. Then he pushes his face up to Meg's face. He opens his eyes wide to take in the full amount of kindness he can now see.

Meg thinks for a moment she is going to get a kiss and pushes her lips out, ready. However, to her disappointment, the kiss doesn't come. Perhaps the kiss might come another time, maybe when they have known each other better.

Jimmy keeps on looking intently into Meg's eyes. Suddenly he knows that everything will be just right. He opens his mouth ready to sing. Immediately the tune of the hymn they sang that morning comes into his head. It is the first verse of 'Morning Has Broken'. He takes a big breath and breathes out the words to the beat of the hymn.

Ganma ehind er sea.
Ganma ehind er sea.

It is very soft and quiet and Meg strains to hear it.

'Can yer sing it louder?'

Jimmy stands on tiptoe so that the air in the sky will go down to his toes. He takes the biggest breath he has ever taken and sings.

Ganma ehind er sea.
Ganma ehind er sea.

'Jimmy, is yer saying yer grandma's behind the sea?'
  'Eese.'
  'Yer what?' asks Meg.
  'EESE!'
  'Oh, Iz knows it. Yer saying yes.'
  'EESE! EESE!'

Jimmy did good.

Jimmy did good.

He is so happy that he jumps and claps four times in the air. But more amazing still is that Meg has understood him.

He has done well and he knows he has done well. And it has been Meg who has helped him. And she is grinning at him now, knowing she has done something special. Jimmy is so happy, more than he has been for a long time. He is speaking with his tongue voice! His purple-song words tell him again he has been a good boy.

Jimmy did good.

Jimmy did good.

Meg catches his joy, but has no idea how Grandma has got where she is and where exactly behind the sea she is! She senses that her reasoning is mixed up, but then she often feels muddled up. Maybe when he sees the sea he will be able to tell her which bit of it they have to look behind.

'Jimmy, when we get to the sea yer needs to show me which bit to look behind, right, have yer got that?'

Jimmy does get it. He looks straight at Meg and shakes her hand four times. Meg grins back. At last Jimmy has held her hand!

The moment when Jimmy first sees the sea, the impact on him is gigantic. This is the biggest hole he has ever seen. And the moment he sees the sea it begins to sing its own wave-splashing song.

Jimmy see a big, big, big, big hole.

A big, big, big, big sea hole.

Nothing matches it in its enormity. Every breaker, smell and sound is astounding. The sea whispers its beauty in its own perfect melody and takes over his body. It hushes him into a reverent silence. For Jimmy, this is like being in church. This is like being part of the heartbeat of the universe. His soul absorbs the magnitude of it all, and as he watches the sea move and dance, he wants to join it. He wants to be a part of it forever. And then, in a wonderful way for just one moment in time it becomes *his* sea and it sings to its new owner:

Jimmy has a sea. Jimmy has a sea. Jimmy has a sea.

Then Jimmy cries. Great big sea-tears; little-boy-lost tears and emerging-man tears surge down his face and wash his throat.

He covers his face with his hands; his fingers spread out in a fan-shape to mop them all up. He tastes their saltiness.

Then, suddenly, it is dusk, and Jimmy can now see through the fan the beginning of the end of the day. He watches in awe as large chunks of peach clutch tightly to light shades of grey and descend gracefully from the sky, then drop into the sea. It is difficult to know now which is sea and which is sky as both are blending together.

He holds his breath, conscious that if his heart should beat the noise will frighten it all away. He doesn't want that; he wants all of it to last forever. It is a perfect moment.

Meg has been sensible not to speak or even to ask questions. She learnt the hard way when she was in the workhouse that you don't ask questions when human beings cry. However, her practical nature is now taking over.

'It's gonna get dark, Jimmy. Jimmy, Iz don't like the dark.'

'Ark,' replies Jimmy, and he cries again at the relief that he has said a word he doesn't like; and by saying it, it has stopped the bad word from going red in his head.

'Jimmy, us can come next Sunday.'

That's when it all comes back to him, the reason why he is looking at the sea. And seeing it all has been like church. And he has always gone to church with Grandma. That's when he knows he will have to wait until next Sunday to look for Grandma. Sunday will be the day he will find her.

The following Sunday finds Jimmy and Meg back in church. Mary isn't there, and Jimmy has been told there is something wrong with her wee water and her head feels too tight and she has to go to hospital to make it better. He is hoping that the Mary-Jimmy lady gets some good wee water at the hospital and it makes her head feel loose again, like his. The Frieda lady has told him he can give any leftover breakfast porridge to the cat who sometimes sits outside the shop. He likes to have jobs to do, as Grandma gave him jobs to do. And the Frieda lady has the same colour hair as Grandma. And the Frieda lady has told him he can choose some biscuits from the shop for the Frieda lady to take to the Mary-Jimmy lady. He likes this idea. He doesn't want the Mary-Jimmy lady to forget him.

Jimmy likes the church the moment he sees it again. He liked it last week because the sun shone through the window on to his toes. This time he likes it because it has a big blue clock on it and anything that has a clock that big has to be good.

The inside of it is good too, as it has pictures on the windows which makes him think about his own picture book. For a moment the memory that it is gone makes him feel sad, but then he looks up to see the top of the church and is immediately struck by the pattern of the roof. It has an impressive number of lines which all seems to disappear in a round bit in the middle. They are nearly as good as the lines he saw in the train-sleep world; lines make him feel safe.

But the one thing that he likes the most, because it makes him feel cosy inside, are the people singing at the front of the church. He is a bit puzzled that they are all wearing nighties. He wonders if they don't have any other clothes.

He has forgotten that they wore nighties at his church in Hoxton. He was too busy looking at the wings on the angels and wondering if they flew around the church when no one was there...

Jimmy is glad that the Meg lady is staying for Sunday dinner again. He likes the way she asks him to sing when he has something to say. He likes it when she understands him. The Meg lady is a very good, kind lady.

He thinks back to last week's Sunday dinner; it had been very good and filled his toes so much he was able to go and find the sea. Today he will look for the bit of sea where Grandma is and find her behind it and the Meg lady will help him.

Dinner has come again. He has jumped a big time jump. He is glad as it will soon be time to look for Grandma. He eats his dinner so quickly he finishes first. Frieda has given up trying to get him to slow down in case he 'gets indigestion'. She isn't even sure if he knows the word 'indigestion'. In the end she simply lets him be.

For Meg, it is an effort to match Jimmy's eating speed, but she is determined to do it. She is now forming an innocent infatuation for him. In her dreams he has become the film hero and she has taken on the glamour of Dorothy Lamour. Will he hold her hand and gaze into her eyes? She can hardly wait to find out!

'Jimmy, is we going for a walk?' She doesn't wait for an answer but dashes off to find her coat and Jimmy's too.

Jimmy had wanted to say yes to the Meg lady before she dashed off, so he jumps up in the air instead, knocking his chair over in the process.

'Glad you like a walk, lad,' chuckles Michael. 'You've best be off, cos here's Meg with her coat on ready and she's got yours too!'

It is true, she has wasted no time at all in grabbing the coats from the tall cupboard in the passageway behind the shop front.

Jimmy puts his coat on and together they walk through the shop and out into the warmth of the May sunshine. Meg lifts her head and looking at the sky, says, 'God gives us that sun, Jimmy. Iz for us to find the sea.'

They set off together. Jimmy feels so light it is almost like how he felt when he flew his kite lots of clock-days ago. He runs as he has never run before. Fortunately for Meg, she manages to keep up with him. She learnt how to run fast in the workhouse. It was a way of preventing being walloped across the earhole, and staying out of trouble.

But today her heart is as light as Jimmy's.

Jimmy flying to the sea.

Jimmy flying in the pavement.

Jimmy jump to the sea.

Jimmy jumps and runs.

In no time at all they reach the road that leads to the sea. And the sea is still there at the end of the road. The one he saw last Sunday, still there waiting for him. One last jump and run and he will see it all. He puts all his energy in to his last jump, then his last run and then, without any warning to Meg, he suddenly stops. This isn't what he had expected to see.

When Jimmy had seen the sea for the first time he had seen nothing else but the sea. Hills, sand and any object – big or small – hadn't existed. His first encounter with the sea had been so overwhelming that he had seen nothing else. But as he looks at the sea today, his vision widens in full detail. The view is a grim one. His eyes are now absorbing the reality of the Dover coastline, a coastline at war. The soft scene of the previous Sunday now looks hard and brittle; it springs out at him and cuts into his soul.

Jimmy see sea fence.

Jimmy not like sea fence.

The sight of a fence of barbed wire winding along the seafront with the sole purpose of stopping the enemy from entering the country is a shock for Jimmy. In Jimmy's eyes it goes on forever and seems to climb the hills themselves. He feels wretched. How is he to get past it? How is he going to get behind the sea if he can't get anywhere near it?

This passive defence, although essential for the safety of innocent human beings, means nothing to him.

This is his worst moment, worse than the blood-smeared rabbit and continuous red words and not being able to talk. This is devastation. What is he to do? The shock is so overpowering he can't bear to look at it. He sinks to his knees and opens his mouth; the wail that comes forth strikes Meg between the eyes and scatters seagulls away to inland places.

'Jimmy, what's up? Is you ill?' she cries, bending down to look at him.

They had started out together in a happy state of mind. Jimmy had been so happy to walk and jump. They were going to the sea and it was meant to be a happy afternoon.

'Jimmy, can yer tell me? Iz needs to know. Can yer sing me it?'

No reply.

'Is he alright – your friend, I mean?'

The unexpected voice of a man behind her makes her jump. The passer-by continues, 'He seems to be upset about something.'

'Yes, no, don't know. Jimmy, what's wrong, is yer ill?'

Jimmy hears Meg's words but they seem to be coming from a long way away. He wants to call out that he isn't ill, but can't. It is then he realises that something which he believed had gone forever returns once more. It is the bad red words, and they are snatching away his ability to speak.

The red words taunt him, accuse him and shame him.

Jimmy can't go to sea. Silly Jimmy.

They get bigger.

JIMMY CAN'T GO TO SEA. SILLY JIMMY.

They become bigger and faster.

SILLY JIMMY. SILLY JIMMY. SILLY JIMMY.

He wants to wail again like he has just done. He wants to howl, bawl, scream, shriek and yell that he needs to get behind the wire thing. He opens his mouth to tell the man who is now kneeling down next to him, but all he can manage is an empty breath moan. The moan is so eerily silent that no one hears it.

If he had known then that there were fighting men not many miles away from him who would have liked to have been where he is – a place which is behind the sea for them, where their womenfolk can be found doing everyday ordinary things – it might have made him feel better, or at least less lonely. But for Jimmy, he is the only person in the whole wide world who is lonely. No one but him knows grief as he does now, no one at all.

Meg is now looking helplessly at the stranger. He returns the same helpless look, neither knowing quite what to do next. Eventually the stranger speaks: 'Well, we can't leave him here.'

It is an obvious statement, but Meg jumps at it as though she has been given a prophetic message. She bends down and shouts in Jimmy's ear.

'Jimmy, is yer coming back?'

'Does he live with you, then?'

'Yes, no. Well, Iz means he lives in the shop.'

'Is he quite, well, you know?' The stranger looks embarrassed at his own words. However, the meaning is quite lost on Meg.

'Jimmy is Jimmy.' It is the only answer she can think of. Her only concern now is to get Jimmy safely back to the shop.

'Well, I reckon we can both heave him up if we try.'

They try but he is a dead weight and resists being moved. The whole thing looks hopeless.

'It's no use; I don't think he wants to be helped.'

'Jimmy, is you coming? Iz told you before, Iz don't like the dark.'

At this, Jimmy moves a little. He has heard the word 'dark' from somewhere in a tunnel and it has frightened him.

'Come on, old chap, back to it. There's a war on, you know.'

The result of these words on Jimmy is electrifying. The tunnel suddenly goes away and unexpectedly the world takes on a tinge of purple.

Jimmy hear waron. Jimmy like waron.

170

Then, like a scene from a film, the memory of building the new hoose with the Eddy man and hearing about the waron, which he had thought was like a lion, comes back to him. But how has the waron got here? Has it hidden itself on the train? But more importantly, will the waron help him to find Grandma? Maybe if he finds the waron it will bite the metal thing and make a big hole for him to get through. This is better.

And now the waron is singing to him and filling his head holes with good thoughts. He will come back next week when the dark has gone and the sun is standing up in the sky. He will find the waron and get it to make a hole for him so that he can get to the sea and look for Grandma. He will go now. Go with the Meg lady. Go with the man. Go back to the hoose in the sky.

It is a weary trio who make their way back to the shop.

'Now then, Meg, why was Jimmy unhappy about seeing the sea today?' asks Michael. 'He loved it last week and came back all smiles.'

Tea is over, eaten in silence. Explanations will come later. Jimmy isn't here; the events of the Sunday afternoon have exhausted him. He has managed a bit of Sunday tea – Spam sandwiches and tinned fruit – but then at Michael's suggestion has gone to bed.

'Iz know that one, Iz knows it.'

'Alright, Meg, but just say it as it is.'

'He thinks his Grandma is behind the sea. He sed it, whenever it woz, can't rember when. And he woz happy when he saw the sea first time, but Iz don't know why he goes all peculiar today!'

'Oh no, I've just remembered,' Frieda interjects. 'She's dead – the grandma, I mean. There was a gas explosion in the house

171

and she was killed outright. Jimmy only survived because he was on the way to the toilet at the bottom of the garden. Mary told me all about it last night when I went to visit her. I meant to tell you, Michael, but I had a resident die at work, lovely lady, eighty-six she is – was. I found her on the floor and it fair upset me.'

Frieda is now looking upset and wiping her eyes on a hanky, the bit that has her initials on.

Meg too begins to cry. The shock has unnerved her. She has seen so many people die at the workhouse and has grown up knowing all about death. It has helped to know that dead people are now in heaven. At least heaven is an escape from the workhouse. The thought of Jimmy looking for someone who is really dead is shocking.

Michael doesn't cry. He is puzzled rather than shocked.

'So why does he think Grandma is alive, then? And why the sea? I don't know what's going on in that lad's head, but I wonder if he will be better off in a home.'

'No, Michael, Mary brought him here to us. There must be a reason for all of this.' Frieda has found her voice and is quick to reply. Meg, however, is appalled at the very suggestion.

'You're not to put him in one of them places. Iz knows, Iz bin in one. You're not, you're not.'

And with that final command she jumps up from her chair and runs out of the room. For a few moments neither of them speaks. Each of them has their own thoughts. Finally Michael breaks the silence.

'It's best if we leave it for today.'

It's Michael's last word for now. Frieda knows it and nods. She knows when she's beaten.

It takes a good few days for Jimmy to recover; being strong, his body recovers before his mind. Michael notices the difference in Jimmy and is at a loss to know what to do about it. His thoughts about Jimmy's future go one way, then another. Many times he shakes his head at the quandary he is in. The only thing he is certain of is that they can't let Jimmy go in to an institution at the moment.

Meg's outburst has affected him deeply and he really doesn't want to upset her. He hadn't realised it until now, but Meg has become the daughter he and Frieda never had.

A few days later Jimmy is sufficiently recovered to help again in the shop. Frieda has taken over the running of it as Michael has gone down with a cold. The nursing home hadn't been keen for her to take time off, but it can't be helped. As she said to Michael one day: 'Well, at least I can take it as holiday pay.'

'Sure you can manage?'

'Yes, Jimmy can still do his jobs and Meg can stack the shelves.'

'Well, mind your back. All that lifting you do at work. We're not getting any younger.'

'Hark at you. What about all that digging you do down at the allotment?' chuckles Frieda.

'Well, watch yourself, girl.'

And so it is that on the first day Frieda is behind the counter, Old Doug – who is a regular customer – comes into the shop. He has waited outside until the shop emptied. It is his usual custom. Old Doug doesn't like talking to people. They are too nosey for his liking.

Frieda knows Old Doug well. In fact, she has known him since a child when she had been taken to visit him by an elderly

Victorian aunt who was known for her philanthropic deeds in the local community. 'Taken' had been the word; Aunt Alice never tolerated the word 'no'. Children who said no had no tea, and Aunt Alice's teas were worth a visit to a 'character', as she described him.

Frieda thinks about the first time she visited his country cottage. It had been scary for a child of seven. The road had been so dark. The pine trees that joined together across the road had looked like a wizard's heavy hat. The moment they had arrived there had been stern instructions by Auntie to shake hands properly with the gentleman. The word 'properly' had meant a polite how-do-you-do as well as a handshake; and all of it had to be done with a correct eye-contact smile. She had wondered then if he was a goblin. He still reminds her of a goblin even now.

'The usual, Woodbine?' she asks.

A grunt is all that she gets in reply.

She turns to the shelf that has an array of cigarettes on when suddenly there is a thudding noise and a scream from Meg. Frieda turns round quickly. Old Doug has collapsed and is now lying on the floor. There is no movement from his sprawled body.

'Fetch a blanket, Meg!' Frieda calls out urgently.

Meg goes and returns with a blanket. She hands it to Frieda.

Frieda bends down to put the blanket over Old Doug's lower body and then feels for his pulse. She can't find one. She knows he's dead. She has seen many old folk die at the nursing home but she doesn't want to frighten Meg. However, Meg knows the truth.

'He's deaded, Iz knows it.'

'Now, calm yourself Meg; you just stay with him while I ring for the ambulance.'

Old Doug is definitely dead. The still body, the staring eyes say it all. Death has come swiftly, and fortunately Old Doug has felt no pain.

Just then Jimmy comes in with a large cardboard box of tea. The sight that meets him startles him. There is something wrong, but he doesn't know what it is and red words in his mind are now speaking his unease:

Jimmy see man on the floor.

Jimmy not like it.

Jimmy see Meg lady not like it.

'Jimmy, he's deaded; I knows he iz.'

Jimmy doesn't move. He has no idea what Meg is talking about.

CHAPTER
15

'Jimmy, look at him, he's deaded. Jimmy, yer knows about deaded?'

Deaded? Jimmy thinks about 'deaded', but it means nothing to him; it has no colour or music.

Meg sees the puzzled look on Jimmy's face.

'It's like when yer body stops working and yer stop seeing stuff.'

Jimmy doesn't move. The thought that his body and especially his legs can't work any more immobilises him.

'Jimmy, you have to see deaded.'

Jimmy doesn't see Frieda come back into the shop behind him, but intuitively he knows she is there. So when she speaks it is no surprise.

'Jimmy, you must look.'

Jimmy doesn't move. Sad red words are filling his mind:

Jimmy sees sad faces. Jimmy not like sad faces.

But he knows he has to look; he hears the instructions given to him and he knows he has to obey. Meg and Frieda watch to see what he will do next. It is like watching a film with its grey scene of death.

One step at a time he edges his way forward until he is beside the body. Meg then reaches out and takes his hand.

'Yer needs to look, Jimmy. Jimmy, yer needs to look at the eyes. There're not moving, the dark is all over im.'

Fortunately, Jimmy understands Meg. He has seen the little hair-eye bits on people's eyes move up and down. Has the man kept his eye bits from not moving to stop the dark from coming in? He has to know, so he looks down.

For a moment Jimmy thinks the man is staring at something on the floor. He looks all around but there is nothing on the floor to be seen. He then looks back at the man. He stares into his eyes for a long time. He isn't frightened, just puzzled, and his mind isn't coming up with any words to help him. The blankness of the man's eyes match the blankness he feels. He has known good eyes and bad eyes and happy eyes and sad eyes and closed eyes and open eyes. But this is something new; why don't the hair-eye bits on the man move?

Both Meg and Frieda sense it is not a time for words, and wait to see what he will do. But Jimmy does nothing and continues staring. The silence in the shop is now becoming uncomfortable and Meg begins to feel its clamminess. She can see Jimmy's fingers begin to twitch. She watches as he begins to curl and uncurl them. She knows he is trying to understand what he sees in front of him. Reaching out for his hand, she twirls him round to face her.

'Jimmy, he can't see now. He can't see nobody.'

Just then the ambulance arrives, breaking the silence that has now settled between the three of them. Frieda goes to open the shop door to let the ambulance man in. Meg takes hold of Jimmy's arm and gently leads him to one side of the shop. Jimmy stares as the man on the floor is taken away, he hopes his eyes will get better soon.

The atmosphere in the shop is now lightning-electric; each person in the room senses it palpitating with glued blobs of emotion. It had only been one cranky old man, but it is a war death and, for Frieda, a reminder of how war can wipe out thousands of people.

A number of people are now waiting to come into the shop. Some passers-by have stopped to watch the tragic scene. Some have now gone but others stay outside to have a good gossip. Frieda decides to close the shop. She is in no mood for gossipers.

It is Meg who speaks first, as she feels it is her job to make sure Jimmy understands about death.

'He's gone now, Jimmy. That means he won't be better again cos he's deaded all over his body. Do yer get what I'm sayin? Jimmy, do yer get it? He's gone. He's not better.'

Jimmy looks back at Meg and sees the goodness in her eyes again and feels happy about that, but the words she has spoken don't really make sense. The only words he has absorbed are 'gone' and 'better', as they were at the end of all the other words. There were too many of them for him to take in. And his mind-words have deserted him too; his mouth-voice won't work today.

'Jimmy, they will take him to church in a box, then they will dig a hole and puts him in. That's what they do, Jimmy, to deaded people.'

Meg leans forward and pushes her face up to Jimmy's. Jimmy doesn't mind this; it is a normal thing to do when you are finding out things.

'Jimmy, do yer get it?' she repeats. She is beginning to feel desperate as she sees nothing in Jimmy's face to suggest he has got it.

Jimmy continues staring. He isn't sure what he is supposed to get as there is nothing in Meg's hand to get. He bends his head down to check if there is anything in his own hands, but there is nothing there either.

Then it is as though his mind races forward and an array of words he hears form themselves into a queue:

Gone Better Church Box Hole

They have no colour; but this happens sometimes when he is thinking hard. Then the first four words rearrange themselves in a bright purple sentence: the man has gone to church in a box to get better. That is it.

Gone to church in a box to get better!

Jimmy likes this idea. He likes churches; they are good picture and singing places. A slow side-smile elongates his face and Meg notices it at once.

'Jimmy, yer got it now.' And she gives him her own two-missing-teeth grin.

But then Jimmy's smile goes. There is one more word which hasn't joined the queue with the others.

Hole?

Meg sees the smile disappear and wonders how much he has really understood.

'Jimmy, yer must get it all. Jimmy, yer must get it.'

She is becoming weary. The events of the day have taken their toll and she wonders if she is wasting her time. She is becoming desperate and she is running out of ideas, but unknown to her, Jimmy's mind hasn't stopped working.

Hole. Why will the man get better in a hole? He is puzzled for the third time that day. He thinks hard. Then something in his brain connects together. He remembers holes in his garden and how the cat liked making them and how he stirred the wet, cool earth in them. It had been fun. That is it: the man is going to make holes when he gets better. Then it will be fun for the man too. Now the words make sense and they are dancing a happy purple jig:

Jimmy like fun holes. The man like fun holes.

And at last Jimmy's face clears. Meg sees it and claps. Jimmy claps too. Meg is now sure Jimmy understands about death. She has done well, she thinks. However, without realising it, Meg has omitted one important fact: she hasn't told Jimmy that his Grandma is dead.

It's surprising how the subconscious mind works even when its owner is fast asleep. Meg suddenly wakes up at two forty-six in the morning with an immediate realisation that she has missed something. What is it? Then as she lies there, wide awake, it comes to her.

She shouts out her memory.

'Dratted, I niver told Jimmy his grandma is deaded! Iz all arms and legs again.'

CHAPTER
16

When Jimmy wakes up the following day he feels better than he has done for a long time. It is a beautiful May day and the events of yesterday have blurred away into a big swirl. His mind has selected not to remember them. There is no reason why he should. It hasn't impacted his life.

The first thing he hears is a lone blackbird singing in the sky. He begins to think about birds. The cat sometimes brought birds home for him to play with, but they were always asleep and he hadn't wanted to wake them up. It would have been nice if they had been awake, as he could have talked to them.

He knows they talk because the hymn says so. It is the hymn Meg sang when he wanted to say where Grandma was. It makes him feel extra happy today. So he jumps three happy jumps to the bedroom window and opens the curtains. He can just see the blackbird sitting on the tree which has long, white flowers on it. This is his favourite tree because it always waves to him when it is windy.

He is so excited to see the bird he jumps three more happy jumps.

But now it is time to do his usual morning jobs. So he does them in the exact same order as he has always done. After breakfast he finds his way to the shop to start the day. He looks around him to see Michael but he isn't here.

Michael's cold has got onto his chest and, as he is prone to chest infections, he has decided to take to his bed. Frieda has gone out to post a letter and Meg has not arrived yet.

The quietness must mean it's Sunday. And Sunday is looking for Grandma day. He can't remember if he has gone to church with Meg; maybe he has. Maybe his mind has done a jump again. He doesn't mind when his mind does jumps, jumps are fun. Maybe if he goes to the sea, Meg might be there waiting for him.

Then out of the blue he remembers the waron.

He wonders if the waron has bitten the metal thing yet and made a big hole for him to get through. And once more the waron is singing to him and filling his head with good thoughts of finding a hole.

Jimmy look for the hole.

Jimmy find the waron hole.

But how to get to the sea? he wonders. He doesn't know the way. The last time he went to the sea, there had been lots of roads and corners and there was a lady with a dog. There is nothing for it; he has to find the sea by himself. So, summoning up the courage he has started to have more frequently these days, he walks to the door, opens it and then looks both ways. This is what he does when he crosses the road on his own. It's to keep his toes safe.

It is the best thing he could have done because coming round the corner is the lady with the dog.

Jimmy see the dog lady. Jimmy see the dog lady.

Jimmy follow the dog lady. Jimmy follow the dog lady.

He is so happy to see the dog lady that he gives three happy jumps which land him a little way onto the pavement. Then he stands still. The dog lady is approaching at a slow speed due to her inquisitive dog who wants to smell every new thing that has arrived overnight.

He doesn't mind dogs but they aren't as much fun as cats. Dogs don't make good holes. He really wants this dog to stop smelling everything it sees. He needs the lady and the dog to walk past him so he can follow them.

Maybe if he walks a little way round the corner and waits there, he thinks, he will see the way the lady and the dog go. Jimmy's mind races with excitement and his own time clock speeds up.

But the dog's mind hasn't; every new smell just has to be investigated and so it is that Jimmy finds he is safely around the corner long before the dog and its owner are anywhere near it. There is nothing for it; he will have to stand still and wait.

To pass the time he looks down his legs to check to see if his toes are still there. He needs them today. He needs them to walk to the sea with. That is when he notices a small crease at the knee on one trouser leg. He bends down to look closer at it. The crease looks a bit like one of the lines on Grandma's face.

He feels the crease's thinness; he likes the way it melts back into the smoothness of the trouser material. He tries rubbing the crease with his longest finger. It has to be his longest finger so it will match the length of the crease. Then he turns his finger over to see if the crease has transferred onto it. It hasn't. He is so busy doing this that he hasn't seen the dog bounding round the corner, followed by its puffing owner hanging onto its lead.

'Oh, it's...' Rusty's owner peers closer at Jimmy. 'Yes, you was the young man – um – Jimmy, who was out with the Meg... oh it was when? Well, not to worry, the memory's not what it is.'

Jimmy is so pleased to see the dog he jumps up and down three times and grins at it. Rusty's owner is startled by the sudden jumping but then remembers a neighbour telling her that Michael has taken on a lad who is 'a bit simple'. Those words had been enough for her to feel sorry for Jimmy. She had replied, 'Well, they are often harmless, a bit like children in their minds.' The neighbour hadn't said anything back but had looked disdainful.

She peers once more at Jimmy. The new cataract which has formed on one eye has forced her to check twice everyone she thinks she knows.

'Well, young man, Rusty he does like you; so we shall go on our walk to the seafront together; if it is a run well Rusty likes that.'

Jimmy grins again. The idea of running, walking and jumping with Rusty sounds so good that he jumps three jumps again, which makes Rusty bark. Then they are off: dog and male human together, followed by a puffing female human owner. All three find themselves at the sea coast in record time.

The sea has a lacklustre look about it today. Its dullness reflects an absent sun (which after a brief appearance has decided to go in) and the colourless waves echo back a ragged grey sky. At first Jimmy doesn't know what to make of it. It still looks majestic, but there is something sad about it. However, that doesn't take away his desire to get behind it. Grandma is there and he has to find her; he must find her today, she has been gone a long time. And although the sea is grey, its song is deep purple and each incoming wave rises and falls in three-part rhythm:

Grandma behind me.

Grandma behind me.

Grandma behind me.

Look Jimmy look.

Look Jimmy look.

Grandma behind me.

The line of barbed wire is still there but Jimmy isn't shocked to see it this time. The ripe thought that the waron may have made holes in it buoys him up.

Fortunately, Rusty is also interested in the barbed wire – but at ground level there are lots of exciting smells to investigate and spend time sniffing. This is perfect for Jimmy. All he has to do is look for a hole every time Rusty stops at a new smell. Rusty is a good dog; he likes Rusty very much.

Rusty's owner is looking tired; an idea comes in to her mind.

'Tell you what, young man; I'm worn in with all this running. You take Rusty for a walk just for a bit? I sit on this seat and wait and watch. I thinks he needs your young legs this morning.'

For a moment Jimmy is worried that Rusty really needs his legs, and as Rusty has four of his own he can't see why he will need any more. His face clouds over.

'It's alright, he doesn't hurt flies!'

Jimmy is glad that Rusty doesn't hurt flies. Grandma has told him it is wrong to hurt the moving things in the garden. But he is still worried about his own legs.

'Here, take the lead. I trust you. You are good like Meg,' says Rusty's owner, handing the lead to Jimmy.

Jimmy looks for a few moments at his legs of which he still has two, and then at Rusty's. He feels relieved when he sees that Rusty still has the same four doggy legs as before. Meanwhile, Rusty is keen to be off; his front feet are hitting the ground with a jarring movement and his lead is fully stretched.

'Come on, lad, he wants to be off.'

Jimmy do it. Jimmy can do it.

Jimmy take the lead.

And so he does.

In one big scooping movement he takes hold of Rusty's lead and holds it firmly between the fingers of his left hand. In an instant, Rusty is off and immediately Jimmy feels the full effect of flying on the ground. It is exhilarating and wonderful and his breaths shorten and the sea air salts his body and he becomes dizzy with joy. This is elation in its purest form. For a moment he forgets he is supposed to be looking for waron holes until Rusty suddenly stops at an invitation from a new smell. Then Jimmy remembers why he is here.

Rusty is now busy soaking in the delights and smells of stale chips. For Jimmy, this is his chance to examine the barbed wire for holes. He inspects the shape of the wire, and although some of it pokes up at different angles, there are no holes.

Then Rusty, having finished smelling the chips, decides it is time to find the next new smell. This happens more times than Jimmy can count, and at each smelling post Jimmy examines the barbed wire fence; but sadly there are no holes. Not one to be seen anywhere.

Unfortunately, his strange antics have attracted the eyes of a few passers-by and one of them has fetched a policeman. The passer-by indicates where Jimmy is.

'Over there, that man. He's been staring at the barbed wire in a funny way. He keeps on stopping as though he is looking for something.'

The policeman remains stony-faced and marches up to Jimmy, who is now inspecting an interesting, twisted bit of the fence, which has the potential to be a hole. He is so intent on his inspecting that he doesn't hear the policeman's footsteps.

'And what do you think you might be doing?'

The sudden sharp words make Jimmy spin round. Glaring at him is a man wearing shiny buttons on some blue clothes. His narrowed eyes and downturned mouth shows deep, hard contempt of the person he is scrutinising. At once Jimmy catches the bad feeling the man is exuding and his body stiffens.

'Well, what have you to say?'

Jimmy swallows hard in an effort to get rid of the lump which has arrived in his throat. He looks back at the man but it is hard to see his eyes. This isn't good and he has a strong urge to run. Rusty too wants to be off, as he is finished with the latest smell and is straining at the lead to look for the next one.

Just then Rusty's owner arrives on the scene. She has seen what has happened and has come to the rescue.

'He's doing no harm, sir, he's just....' She stops speaking mid-sentence, seeing no softening in the policeman's gaze. In fact, his mouth has downturned a fraction more.

'It looks very fishy to me,' he hisses. 'And you...'

The policeman has no time to finish his sentence, for suddenly a huge noise storms through the air, battering Jimmy with its intensity. It seems to be all around him and it makes his ears hurt terribly. He has no idea what the noise is or where it is coming from. The noise causes Jimmy to let go of Rusty's lead, as if the dog has something to do with it.

'Right, lad, you need to get to an air-raid shelter with us and be quick about it.'

But for Jimmy, this is no time to listen to words he doesn't understand. Without any warning to those who are with him, he suddenly springs forward as though being pursued by a wild animal.

'Come back, you clot,' bellows the policeman, running after him.

Jimmy has no intention of going back. His heart beats wildly and his legs ache, but he can't stop. His immediate instinct is to get away as fast as he can; away from the noise that is droning on and on and wailing all around him. He runs like the wind, leaving the policeman panting behind. Then the noise gets louder. It is coming across the sky and getting louder by the minute. Then suddenly the noise is behind him. And now it is so loud that his legs won't work any more. He throws himself on the ground just glimpsing what the noise thing is. It looks like a bird, but this is the biggest bird he has ever seen. It has a huge body and an arm on either side of it, and it is coming down with a roar that makes him tremble with fright.

Then the biggest shaking noise Jimmy has ever heard pounds all around him and hits the ground some way behind him. It seems for a moment that he is back in his garden at home, striding out to the bumwoodhole. He can also see red sparks in the sky and there is a strange smell just like bonfire night. But he can't see the familiar shape of the bumwoodhole. This is different. Why is it different? Why hasn't he flown in the air like the last time he heard a big bang, and why has he stopped running? And why won't his feet move?

The pounding noise is now going over the town and away from him, but the droning noise is still going on. As he lies there he thinks he feels a lump of fur at his back, pushing against him. For a moment he thinks it is the cat wanting to play holes. Then his mind clears, he turns his head and there stands Rusty, quivering and whimpering with fright. Unknown to Jimmy, Rusty has bolted too at the sound of the siren, leaving his owner behind.

Jimmy reaches his hand out to the terrified animal and in doing so he feels something sticky on his hands. Very slowly he brings his hand to his face and up towards his eyes. Then he sees what it is. It is bright red fresh human blood and it is dripping off his hand. And by the blood lies a severed arm.

Blood on Jimmy. Blood on Jimmy. Blood on Jimmy.

This is bad enough but there is worse to come. In front of him lies the rest of the policeman who had been chasing him. His body has been blown apart by the bomb and Jimmy can now see his bloody remains scattered in horrific bits lying on the road. The sight shocks and sickens him. It has been a direct hit, and across the street a number of buildings are on fire. It has been just one plane, one man – the enemy looking for someone to kill – and he has targeted a running figure in uniform.

It is clear to Jimmy that the policeman's body cannot be mended; there is too much blood and the man's legs and toes are in bits on the pavement. It happened because of a big bang. Is this what happened to Grandma? Big, hard, blood-cold question-words shout in his head:

Grandma in bits?

They then repeat and become bigger and faster.

GRANDMA IN BITS?

Grandma is behind the sea. He knows she is behind the sea. The good people have told him so. The **red words** are **bad**. He will not listen to **bad red words**. But still they come, getter bigger by the minute.

GRANDMA IN BITS? GRANDMA IN BITS?

Then they become a rushing noise in his head and a bad smell is coming through his nose.

Big bad bang.

Big bad smell.

Then a scream grows in his head and pushes itself down to his mouth but his mouth won't open. The scream stays in his head, getting bigger and heavier, clenching his teeth together.

Suddenly the red words begin to wobble.

It is all too much for him.

A door of darkness begins to close in across his eyes.

Then the door shuts.

Meanwhile, in the air-raid shelter, Rusty's owner has been anxiously waiting for the all-clear. When the siren goes off she hurries out of the shelter in the direction of the seafront, ignoring the advice of the wardens on duty. She has to find out what has happened to Jimmy and Rusty.

The sight and smell of what she sees when she gets there shocks her immensely. It is clear that the policeman she had been talking to earlier is dead. She hadn't liked him, but he hadn't deserved this. She wonders if he has a mother or a wife at home. Maybe she will be cooking the dinner and she will have set the table. Maybe there will be rhubarb and custard for pudding. Is she saving thrupenny bits in a jar to go to the pictures once a month, like she does? What a waste of life.

Oh, the waste of it all, she thinks, and there lying still as a statue is Jimmy, with Rusty by his feet.

'Jimmy, you alright?'

At the sound of his name Jimmy opens his eyes and sees a lady with kind eyes looking at him. For a brief moment he doesn't recognise her.

'Jimmy, it's me, the Rusty dog lady! You took him for a walk.'

She doesn't mention the policeman; she thinks it better to leave him out of it.

Very slowly the memories of the morning come back to Jimmy in four different pictures:

The dog.

The sea.

The waron.

No holes.

Then the film continues in one big rush and he remembers the more recent events of the morning. The horrible big bird in the sky that made a big noise and broke the policeman's body and the bad blood all over everything and the big bad smells and the thoughts about Grandma in bits and the scream that got stuck in his teeth and all the big bad red words.

NO. He must stop the film. Close his eyes. Make the pictures go away.

'Is he alright?'

Rusty's owner hasn't heard the light footsteps of the ARP warden approach her. She jumps slightly and turns round.

'Is he hurt? Does he need an ambulance?' the man continues in a somewhat flat voice. He has learnt recently not to show emotion.

'No, I a nurse in the last war. I see no blood and sticky bones!'

The ARP warden doesn't reply. There is really no need to. It is obvious to everyone that Jerry has done his worst.

'Is he a relation of yours?'

'No, he is the not right in the head young man in the corner shop, but he a good man.'

'The corner shop on Abbey Street?'

'Yes,

'So he's not from the hospital, then?' enquires the ARP warden.

'No, he's not one of them in the farm that is funny!'

'Right, then. Do you think you can manage to get him home? There's a lot of clearing up to do here.'

'Yes, I can do it. I can make a cross lady voice, like in war.'

'Please do.'

'Jimmy go to home now!'

The effect on Jimmy is electrifying. He jumps up immediately and stands bolt upright like a soldier who has just received an order from his commanding officer. The suddenness of the action makes him see squiggling lines for a few moments, but when they go he is surprised to see the dog lady, not Grandma.

He thinks he heard Grandma's voice telling him it is time to go home. Maybe Grandma is waiting for him to give him a bath. He knows he has to have a bath as the red blood is still on his hand. He doesn't want the red blood to make his hand go red. That will mean scrubbing it off with a scrubbing brush. He knows about scrubbing brushes. Grandma always uses them on his hands when he has been playing in the cat holes in the garden.

'Well, that did the trick.' The ARP warden has to smile despite the seriousness of the situation.

'Thank you for the help,' replies Rusty's owner, shaking the warden's hand. 'You've got to go now.'

'Yes, there's a lot to do.'

'I know you have a lot to see to, so we will go now.'

'Now, you two walk straight home. Who knows what Jerry has lined up for us next.' And with that parting remark the warden walks away to do his duty.

It is a much more sombre party that walks home than set out earlier. They take a different route to avoid going past the site of the bomb. Jimmy senses he has to go that way as he is leaving the bad smell behind. Rusty trots tentatively behind them. Gone is the earlier inquisitiveness at every smell.

It takes a bit longer to reach Abbey Street but eventually they arrive just as Frieda is opening the front door of the shop. She sees Jimmy first.

'Where the bally heck have you been?'

'Now, before you off him tell, he is shocking!'

'Oh hello, sorry I didn't see you there. Come on in.'

'No thank you, I need to see old man and I will tell you here what it was.'

Frieda listens quietly and without interrupting. For a moment or two she doesn't answer. It is clear to her that Jimmy is becoming more and more preoccupied with this strange notion that his grandma is behind the sea. After a while she speaks.

'Well, thank you for bringing him home safely.'

'No problems with it, dear.' She turns to walk away with the faithful Rusty by her side.

Frieda looks at Jimmy who is now standing like a statue in a museum. Fortunately for Jimmy, the shop is quiet. The air raid has seen to that. But what to do with Jimmy? she thinks. It is becoming clear that the lad isn't going to stop going to the sea. It looks as though Meg's words about death haven't gone in. And that is another problem – where is Meg? 'It never rains but it pours,' she sighs to herself.

Jimmy hears the word 'rain'.

Jimmy likes the word 'rain'.

Rain is like water.

Rain is like bath-time.

Rain is like the wet in the cat holes. He turns his head so that he can look out of the shop window and see the rain. He tries putting his head on one side just in case the rain is still in the sky, but he can't see any. Then he tries putting his head on the other side of his body to see if the rain is coming down the street, but it isn't. He can't understand this. There isn't any rain. Maybe the rain is pouring out of the sky at a different window. He will try his bedroom window, but he has no time as Frieda is speaking.

'Well, then, Jimmy; let's have something to eat and a nice mug of tea. After that we'll have a think together.'

He follows Frieda to the kitchen. He is happy to do this; the rain can wait. Food is good even on bad days. He watches her peel potatoes and put them in a big pan. He is then told he has to wait until they are cooked. Then time does a big jump.

When they are cooked Frieda opens a tin of peas and some tinned meat and puts it on three plates with the cooked potatoes. She takes one plate to Michael, who is now feeling much better and sitting up in bed. Then she returns to the kitchen and sits down next to Jimmy, who by now is tucking in heartily. The death scene from the morning has gone away. The picture-film in his head has come to an end.

After dinner is over they have some tinned peaches for pudding and then finally a mug of tea. Then Jimmy's head begins to wobble down. He knows what to do when this happens; he rests his head on his shoulder and closes his eyes. Soon he is asleep.

For Frieda there is no time to think. Dinner has taken longer than usual. It is time to open the shop again. Jimmy or no Jimmy, she has a job to do and a living to make.

'Have we bitten off more than we can chew?'

It is bed-time and Frieda can't get to sleep. She is thinking about Jimmy. He has spent most of the day sleeping, apart from tea-time, and has gone to bed earlier than usual.

'I was just dropping off,' replies a somewhat irritated Michael.

'Have we bitten off more than we can chew?' Frieda repeats the question. 'About Jimmy, I mean.'

'Not now, love. Whatever it is, talk to you in the morning.'

Frieda hasn't told Michael about Jimmy's escapade. She thinks it wiser not to. But now she has just blurted out what is on her mind without thinking. Daft thing to do, she thinks; maybe Jimmy is beginning to get under her skin too much. And why hasn't Meg turned up? It's a problem she can do without. She will have to sort it out in the morning. It can wait...

CHAPTER
17

Jimmy wakes early the following day due to the fact that he had more than his usual amount of sleep yesterday. The dawn May morning sunshine is the colour of Pease pudding. It makes him feel happy.

His head feels a bit strange but happily yesterday's bad memories have gone in the night. But a good one has stayed with him. He heard Grandma speaking; at least, he thought he had. His head had hurt with a big noise. She told him to do something but he can't remember what it was. He thinks for a long time but the words won't come back.

Then unexpectedly, within the silent space of his room, he hears an urgent whisper.

'*Jimmy, Jimmy.*'

It is Grandma. She is calling to him, but where is she?

He must get up. He must follow the voice. He gets out of bed, puts his slippers on and goes downstairs. It is very quiet. Maybe it is Sunday again. The quietness is good and it makes him feel happy. He finds his way through the shop to the front door and opens it. There are no people in the street and the outside air is a little cool but not cold.

What happens next excites him more than anything that has happened to him so far. There, a few yards in front of him, is Grandma. It doesn't worry Jimmy that she has appeared out of nowhere. She is there, smiling and beckoning him to follow her. He runs to her but she seems to disappear only to appear again a few yards in front of him. All the time she is beckoning him to follow her. He runs again to her but the same thing happens. Then he realises what he has to do. He has to follow; just follow. It is simple.

So that's what he does. He follows the figure he can see in front of him. Sometimes the figure appears out of a wall, sometimes the figure looks pale and he can hardly see her, but that doesn't worry him. It is Grandma and she is moving in front of him and all the time beckoning him to follow her.

Then he reaches the church and the path leading to it. The figure disappears for a moment. Maybe she has gone down the path? He must find out. He runs down the path and there she is, Grandma, clear and real and standing at the church door!

He runs towards her; but like before, she has gone! He has to go inside; perhaps she is waiting for him. His eyes scan the door. He likes the shape of it. It is different from any door he has seen before. He places both hands on it and feels the straight bits. There are three of them. Then he reaches up and feels the round bit at the top. It feels strange because it doesn't go all the way round.

Then he feels the entire middle bit, starting at the top. Eventually he comes to a bit which feels different to the rest of the door. He wraps his fingers around it and tries to turn it – but nothing happens. Then he tries the other way – but again nothing happens. Then he tries pushing it and this time the door opens and he goes inside. The church is empty. He has never seen an empty church before. This is completely new; but what surprises him most is that Grandma isn't here. He had expected to see her but she is gone and he has no idea why.

Is she playing the hide-and-seek game? The church will be an exciting place to hide. Maybe if he looks behind some things he will find her... but where to start? He looks this way and that way. Then he notices that the sun is making a big round shape on the floor in the middle of the church. Maybe if he jumps in the round bit he can twirl round and then he will see if Grandma is hiding in the long seats. So this is what he does, and with one very big jump he lands in the round shape. Then he twirls round three times... but Grandma isn't in any of them.

Then he sees a very small, round shape on the carpet further up. He does three big jumps up to it but it is only a shiny thing he has seen in the shop. Again he looks one way then another, but there is no Grandma. Now there are no round shapes left but there are lots of seats to be looked at. He stands there feeling helpless when suddenly:

'Jimmy, Jimmy.'

There it is again: Grandma's voice. It seems to be coming from the front of the church next to a statue of an angel. The voice is urging him forwards. He has to find her. Then his body grows wings. He is running wildly, helplessly, jumping into corners, searching under the long chairs and behind the big things that hold up the roof. But Grandma isn't here. Where is she? He is getting frightened and he cannot see or hear her.

Where has she gone? And now bad, red words are coming into his head:

Jimmy not see Grandma. Jimmy not see Grandma.

He must sit down; he must go to sleep again, then Grandma will come back like when he had just woken up – but his heart is beating too fast to let him sit down. He must stand still lest it burst. He will stand until the purple words come, telling him what to do. Eventually they come, each one a gentle dewdrop pillowing on a single flower petal.

Jimmy stand still.

Jimmy stand still.

And now filling his head and hushing his body.

Jimmy stand still.

The sweetness of the song calms him down and immediately there comes over him a big tiredness. His head feels floppy. Whether it is from the early start or the lack of food is hard to say, but he knows he has to lie down. But where? Then he remembers:

Jimmy find the floor-sleep pillow.

That is easy; they are with the long chairs. He has seen them before when people in church on Sundays have put their knees on them and gone to sleep. He had gone to sleep once before in church but Grandma had nudged him in the ribs. He had woken up; but then he noticed everyone else had woken up too, so that had been alright.

He bends down and sees there are lots of sleep pillows on the floor near to where he is standing. He picks the nearest one up. Then he sits down on the long chair, twists round and swings both legs onto it. Then he drops the floor-sleep pillow on the long chair by throwing it behind him. Next, he lowers his body so that his head rests on the sleep pillow. He is now lying down with his face looking at the roof of the church. The chair feels stiff on his back like when once he fell asleep on the pantry floor.

Then he bends his legs and turns over so that his back is against the long chair. This is a little bit more comfortable. His eyes begin to feel very heavy, and despite the discomfort of it all, he is soon fast asleep. He is now completely hidden from the world and the war; but worst of all, those who know him.

Earlier that morning, Frieda wakes up at the usual time. The May sunshine streaming into her bedroom lifts her heart and for a moment she forgets there is a war on. She goes to the bathroom and then gets dressed. Michael is still asleep, so she decides to leave him to sleep a bit longer. She then walks the few steps to Jimmy's bedroom. She knocks at his door.

'Jimmy, time to get up.'

No answer.

'Jimmy, time to get up,' she repeats a bit louder.

No answer. This is strange as he usually replies by banging the wall three times. She listens but hears nothing.

She knocks again and waits. Nothing happens, so opening the door a little way, she peeps inside. She can't see him so she opens the door a bit wider. Jimmy isn't there. Where is he? He hasn't gone to the bathroom as the door is open and she can see that it is empty. She is beginning to feel very anxious now. Has he got out in the night and something bad has happened to him? She runs back to her bedroom just as Michael is beginning to open the door from the inside. They collide in the middle.

'Jimmy's not in his room.'

'How do you mean, he's not in his room?'

'He's not in his room, I tell you,' replies Frieda.

'Where is he, then?'

'Well, if I knew that, I wouldn't be standing here talking to you, would I?' And with that she turns and runs down the stairs, leaving her husband to hurry after her.

'He might be in the shop, love!' Michael calls out breathlessly.

'That's where I'm going, you chump!'

Frieda runs in to the shop calling out Jimmy's name, but he is nowhere to be seen. Michael arrives a few minutes later after searching the rest of the building. It is now becoming frighteningly obvious that Jimmy has gone.

'There's nothing for it; I will have to go and look for him,' says Frieda, her voice breaking slightly.

'Look, love, he won't have gone far, and weren't you going to tell me something about Jimmy last night?'

'Yes, I was, and now I feel a bit guilty about it.'

'Look, just tell me the gist of it and then go and find him. I can manage the shop. I was going to say that anyway as I feel a lot better now.'

So Frieda begins her story and gives Michael the bare facts of what happened yesterday. She finishes her story by saying: 'And I also have a problem with Meg. She didn't turn up at all yesterday. It's something else I have to sort out.'

'Well, love, that's your answer. He's probably gone down to the seafront again with Meg.'

Frieda doesn't need any more prompting. She grabs her coat and shoes, puts them on and is out of the door before Michael has the chance to say good luck.

It doesn't take long for Frieda to walk to the seafront. She hasn't been there for a while. She takes in the familiar lie of the coastline as she walks. In front of her is Dover castle, a medieval success, known as the 'Key to England'. Hadn't she heard that so many times from an enthusiastic history teacher at secondary school? Today she feels proud of being British. Here is something permanent. Built by a king, she thinks, built to last, built by craftsmen.

She recalls being told that the castle is the largest in England. Her young brain had appreciated that. She had felt part of its splendour. And around it all spreads a protective wall, strong and true. She muses at the realisation that only twenty-odd miles away across the sea, war rages in Europe. If only the castle wall could protect them from that. If only it could have protected them from yesterday.

However, she is here to find Jimmy. She has to protect him from danger. Her eyes quickly scan what is in front of her, and her first impressions are that he isn't here. But she must check thoroughly; there are a few groups of people about. She wonders how many of them are here to see the after-effects of the bomb. But she isn't here to stare. She must walk the entire seafront and check every possible nook and cranny.

It is a lonely walk, not just because she is on her own but because it becomes increasingly clear to her that there is no Jimmy. Not even in the most unlikely places; she has checked them all. So where to look next? She really has no idea. She thinks of all the places he knows. There aren't that many; apart from the shop and the sea, where else does he know? There is only the church left. Will he go there? It seems a long shot but it is the only place left to try. She will go.

It is a depressed Frieda that turns to walk to the church. She walks with her head down and therefore doesn't notice any passers-by until a familiar voice halts her walk.

'Iz sorry, Iz very sorry, Michael said yer might be here when Iz goes to the shop and Iz very sorry.' It is Meg, breathing out her apologies in one fast garbled sentence.

'Oh, it's you. You made me jump. Now then, young lady, I have a bone to pick with you. What happened –' she demands, but then changes her mind. It will keep for the moment. 'Look, Jimmy has gone missing and I'm going to try the church.'

'Iz knows and Iz very sorry about me not coming to work and Michael sed give Frieda these sandwiches.'

Frieda smiles to herself despite feeling cross with Meg. It is like her thoughtful husband to send sandwiches, knowing she missed her breakfast this morning.

She takes the cloth bag from Meg that contains the sandwiches.

'Right then, my girl, explanations later. You're coming with me to find Jimmy.'

'Right, yes, and Iz very sorry about...'

'Put a sock in it, Meg.'

'Sorry!'

Back at the church, Jimmy wakes up feeling very stiff. He sits up. For a few moments he wonders where he is. He must think. It is very quiet. He isn't in his bedroom at the shop; he is in a big place with lots of long chairs.

Then it comes back to him: he is in a church and he has heard Grandma's voice coming from the front of the church and he has tried to find her. He has to find her. Then the memory comes back of him running wildly, helplessly, jumping into corners, searching under the long chairs and behind the big things that hold the roof up. But Grandma wasn't there. He had become frightened.

Then the sleep song had come and he had gone to sleep on the long chair with the sleep pillow under his head.

But now he is awake and Grandma hasn't come with his clothes and he is still wearing his pyjamas. It is all a big muddle. Maybe if he goes outside the sun will help him think. He likes the sun; he always feels happy when the sun shines. Maybe Grandma is outside in the sunshine.

He wonders how many steps it will take from where he is sitting to the church door. He must stand up; he will count them.

Jimmy count all the steps.

Jimmy can do it.

He counts twenty long steps to the door. This is a good number because it is his age. He finds the big handle on the door by feeling for it, and lets himself out.

And yes, the sun is there and it is waiting for him. He jumps up in the air and feels it fill his ears. In front of him is the path he walked up when he arrived at the church. He looks down the path, but Grandma isn't here. This is puzzling; maybe there is another path he can explore.

Perhaps if he walks around the church he will find one and maybe Grandma will be here. Perhaps she is playing the hide-and-seek game. He must count first before looking for her. He covers his eyes and counts to twenty. Then he opens them and runs down the side of the church, looking in every direction as he runs.

It is a long path and he is out of breath when he gets to the bottom of it. But Grandma isn't here. He tries again with the path that runs along the back of the church. But before he begins to run he hears something, a song-whisper of a voice.

'Over there, Jimmy.'

'Look over there.'

It is Grandma's voice again, softly urging him to stop and look... but where?

'In the grass, Jimmy.'

He turns and faces the grass, then he takes five paces onto the grass, but all he can see are big stone things sticking up. He walks up to them and looks all around them but Grandma isn't here. He tries another, then another. Some of them have flowers underneath them in pretty vases. Some are bigger than others. Some have small pebbles inside a three-line shape. He tries another one and as he looks, a picture-memory comes slowly back to him: Father Keith, an angel, sad faces, a big hole. He thinks about his memory. What does it mean? Why does Grandma want him to look here? And then suddenly two words connect themselves in his head. A blood-red question shouts in his mind:

Grandma hole?

He shakes his head to try to get rid of the bad question, but the picture-memory is becoming more vivid, with real people in front of him. Then suddenly the faces grow out of proportion to their bodies, making them look like grotesque gargoyles.

And from each mouth pairs of twisted lips begin to move. The lips are forming words:

Grandma down in a hole.

And then for the first time in his life a whisper of doubt comes into his mind. It comes as a question:

Grandma body not working?

Does that mean Grandma is like the old man in the shop – 'deaded all over his body'? Meg's words come back to him as clear as the moment they were first spoken, and for the first time he begins to understand them. It is a huge shock. He has to run. He has to get away. He has to escape from deaded. Grandma mustn't be deaded. It would mean no more cat holes, no more Pease pudding, no more plum jam. He has to run away from deaded.

Jimmy run. Jimmy run. JIMMY RUN!

Taking one big deep breath he races up the path to the very end. Then he turns and races down the path at the side of the church. And round once more. He is running away from 'deaded' but it has given chase and is following him.

Then a new thought enters his brain. Will deaded happen to him? Will his body stop working? He must run even quicker and get away from deaded. Then like a bullet spat out from a gun he is off again, but now his worn-out running legs won't synchronise properly. He trips and falls, banging his head on the hard stone path.

The fall shocks him and he lies there for a few moments. He must get up. He mustn't let deaded see him. He must stand up. He must get to the front of the church. He must slide along the wall. He mustn't stand still. He must hide in the church door. He mustn't let deaded see him. He is here, the door is here. The church door will hold him. The church door will hide him from deaded. He leans against it but the door isn't still; he remembers it being still but now it is wobbling. It is moving him and flying away, it is taking Jimmy away, away from the church and the deserted street.

No one sees Jimmy staring into space, his eyes glazing over, his body motionless, his lips smacking together or his eyelids fluttering... no one at all.

The walk to the church doesn't take Frieda and Meg long. Meg keeps on looking at Frieda for some sort of flicker or smile of reassurance, or maybe forgiveness for not turning up for work the previous day, but Frieda remains stony-faced. Her one purpose is to find Jimmy. She will talk to Meg later. Eventually, Meg gives up looking at Frieda, sensing she is in for it.

Meg is the first to spot Jimmy. She speeds up a little and goes ahead in the hope that finding him first will redeem her wrongdoings. Frieda doesn't stop her; it has been a long morning for her aged legs.

'He's there, Iz can just see im. He's standing there. Oo, he's in his pyjamas. Does he know?'

Frieda catches Meg up; and yes, it is Jimmy, slumped but upright by the church door, completely still, like a soldier on guard at Buckingham Palace.

'What do us do?' she continues...

'Let's just call his name and tiptoe up to him. Don't run, it might make him run.' replies Frieda.

Meg frowns, wondering why Jimmy will run away from them; after all, they are his friends. Frieda sees the frown and knows what she is thinking.

'It's because he was very frightened yesterday, the bomb and all that.'

She will leave further explanations until later.

The two ladies reach the path to the church and continue their tiptoe walk towards Jimmy. Has he seen them? It is hard to say, as the expression on his face hasn't changed and his posture remains stiff and lifeless. His head has rolled back slightly and a trickle of white phlegm lines his lips. His eyes are still glazed over.

But then suddenly the absence leaves him, and his body begins to function again. He has been totally unaware of his absence and yet he feels all wrong.

His head aches so very much. And why is he standing outside with his pyjamas on?

He blinks his eyes long and hard to make it all go right again, and then opens them. He is leaning against a church door. He remembers churches; they are nice places with angels in them and sleeping pillows and lots of singing. But he doesn't know why he is here today.

Then slowly the memories of the morning come back to him. He has seen Grandma – or has he heard her? Which is it? He has looked for her but not found her. And there were some bad holes. But what happened after that, he can't remember...

Maybe if he stands still Grandma will find him. He must wait; he doesn't want to miss her. He stands and waits and waits. The only sound he can hear is the wild beating of his own heart. Then after what seems an eternity he sees two

211

figures walking up the path. His eyes feel misty, but through the mist he can just make out the Meg and Frieda ladies who are now hurrying towards him. Meg speaks first,

'Jimmy, is yer alright?'

Jimmy hears the words clearly enough but his brain cannot take them in. They sound kind but he is still thinking about Grandma. She hasn't come. Maybe she has sent the Meg and Frieda ladies to bring him to her. Then his memory fuddles over and goes blank.

'Jimmy, is yer alright?' Meg repeats.

'Now then, Meg, let's not bombard him with questions.'

Frieda studies Jimmy's face, looking for any emotion that will give her a clue as to why Jimmy is here. But all she can see is a vacant expression. This worries her more than if he had looked frightened or confused. Instinctively she reaches up her cardigan sleeve for a hanky to wipe the dried phlegm... Then, walking to the bin on the side of the right-hand path, she throws it away and returns to Jimmy and Meg. During this time Jimmy doesn't flinch or move at all but keeps on staring at Meg. Meg stares back, not quite knowing what to do next.

'Can I help?'

Meg and Frieda jump at the sudden voice and turn round to see who it is. It is the vicar, who has come to the church to search for some missing sermon notes. His raised eyebrows display the surprise he now feels at seeing a young man standing by the church door in his pyjamas. The two women who are with the young man seem at a loss as to what to do next.

Jimmy too has heard the voice and, thinking it is the policeman who has come back as a goblin to scare him, faints clean away into Meg's arms.

CHAPTER
18

The vicar offers to take them all home. It is something of a struggle to support a recovering Jimmy to the waiting car, but they manage it between them. They get in themselves and sit in silence, not wanting to upset him. On their way home, Jimmy's vulnerability begins to remind them of their own. For the vicar, Jimmy reminds him of when as a child he had lost his younger brother, Stevie, whom he loved very much. Stevie was a small child with large horse-brown eyes that mirrored their mother's. He was a gentle and sensitive child who never knew good health. But it is the cough he remembers most – persistent and fretful, causing him to wheeze a lot.

Their dad had said Stevie couldn't kick a ball around outside in the backyard because 'it be his lungs, lad'. Then Stevie had died and the death certificate said 'failure to thrive'. Just an innocent little boy with an illness no one could put a name to. Even now he doesn't know what 'failure to thrive' means. Maybe one day someone will give it a name, one that means something.

Frieda is thinking about the time when she almost confessed to Michael that maybe she has been wrong about Jimmy, and that he should go into a home. But seeing how frightened he looked at the church has made her feel guilty that she has even thought of sending him away. She now has to look after him more than ever.

Meg, like the vicar, has also been visited from the past. It is always the same memory. She is back in the workhouse once more and she feels ugly. There had been people who had called her names, just because her legs and arms are thin. She had felt unloved. She had wandered around aimlessly, trying to find someone who would like her and talk to her in a kind voice. Those years had been the dark night of her soul. Maybe Jimmy will love her. Maybe when he is better he will love her.

But today, at least for Jimmy, there is no head space for love. Yesterday's events are tangling themselves up with his most recent ones and are entering a big church that has an angel in it.

It has been a morning of ghosts for everyone...

Meg is now looking sheepish as she knows what is coming next. She is seated at the kitchen table with Frieda, eating a somewhat unusual breakfast comprising of Michael's sandwiches, which they hadn't had time to eat earlier, and some hot soup. Jimmy has been given some porridge, toast and tea and has been packed off to bed. Neither lady has spoken to each other during the meal.

Meg knows she will have to come clean now. She hates silences; she had too many of them in the workhouse. She swallows the last bite of her sandwich and inhales deeply, anticipating Frieda's wrath. She begins to speak, but Frieda is in no mood for Meg's 'sorries'.

214

'Right, now then, young lady, why didn't you come to work yesterday?' she demands.

A pale red blush grows on Meg's cheek and becomes brighter. One single tear births itself in her left eye. She rubs it away roughly with one finger.

'I shud av teld Jimmy that his grandma is deaded, yer knows, when Old Doug died and I said about deaded, but then, well, my mind can't do lots of thinks. And also it well was... the usual...' her voice trails off with embarrassment. 'You know, that thing wot happens to women, and it hurted a lot.'

Meg's blush grew redder.

'Now, don't start doing that again. You can't have days off because you're a woman. I told you this last time it happened. You just have to get on with it like every other woman does. Take some aspirin. And now my girl, you've got a job to do in the shop.'

The following week goes by quickly. Michael gets better and goes back to serving in the shop and Frieda goes back to her own job at the nursing home. Meg settles down again and Jimmy recovers physically (at least, that's what those around him think) from his earlier ordeal.

However, he doesn't feel right about himself. He can't remember the episode at the church; his mind hasn't recorded that particular event, but it has left him feeling all wrong. But he can't put a name to what it is. It is as though something about him or stuff around him isn't the same.

The memory of the possibility of Grandma's death has gone completely and his thinking has regressed to believing that Grandma is still alive. The desire to find Grandma is as strong as ever and yet it is different. His one hope to find her is battling with something new, a conflicting idea that somehow he has got it all wrong.

Yet it is hard for him to own these puzzling thoughts. Everything has gone wrong.

Maybe the fact that he can remember the earlier episode of the bomb and the death of the policeman has confused him as to who the bad people are and who the good people are. He has always thought that policemen are good people and yet one of them had chased him.

This is a dead time for Jimmy; it feels as though he is waiting for something to happen. And people around him have stopped smiling and he doesn't know why. He has seen shakes of heads and murmurings of bad things happening in the world from customers in the shop.

The truth is that the news about the war isn't good. The newspapers are reporting on increasing fears about an invasion and the enemy is getting nearer. Is Great Britain in danger of being taken over by the Germans? It is a frightening thought.

CHAPTER
19

Michael is feeling bored.

By lunchtime he had served the few customers who had wanted to talk to him. It had been gratifying to know that they had missed him when he'd been unwell.

He had sent Meg and Jimmy to do some cleaning in the back to 'keep busy'. Meg had gone willingly, happy at the thought that she will be alone with Jimmy. Jimmy had been puzzled as to whose back needed cleaning, but he had gone anyway.

The shop is now empty.

Michael finishes his last sandwich and drinks his tea. He then picks up the newspaper and begins to read. The news isn't good. Hitler's armies are gaining the upper hand. The enemy, with their air superiority and tenacity, are advancing through Europe at an alarming rate. France is in serious trouble. Holland has already surrendered earlier in the month and now Belgium has surrendered too.

He thinks about his two sons who were killed in the last war, and shudders. Just how many young lives have been lost in this present war? And how many more are going to lose their lives? He feels helpless thinking about the enormity of it all – and all because of one madman who wants to own the world; just one madman with a moustache...

Back in Hoxton, Father Keith reads the same account in his newspaper. His response is to go to his study and pray. He also says a prayer for a young man named Jimmy, wherever he is now.

Eddy Woodhouse reads the same thing in his newspaper. His first thought is to think about the wife he has loved and lost. He guessed early on she had gone to Dover. There is nowhere else she could have gone, having no other relations in the world.

He had wanted to go after her but couldn't. How could he expect her to come home after what he has done? The shame he felt has been excruciating. He has been to the doctor about his headaches and they have turned out to be not much at all, just a vitamin deficiency. He has been given medication to take for them. And now he just hopes that Mary and Jimmy will be safe. At Dover they are nearer to France and an invasion might harm them first.

The country now holds its breath. The next few days will be crucial for the safety of many vulnerable people.

Tuesday, 28 May 1940
'Right, Michael, we have to do our bit.'

George, Michael's 'boat mate', has just charged into the shop, causing the door to bang behind him, and is now addressing his friend in his down-to-earth, direct way. He has come straight to the point without any preamble. Michael is used to this, so doesn't bat an eyelid. It is late afternoon and he is just about to close the shop.

George leans against the counter and waits until Michael turns the 'closed' sign on the shop door. Michael then walks back to where George is standing. He can't help but notice the pinched look on his friend's already thin face, as well as the overbright look in his eye. It makes him feel uneasy.

George doesn't wait for Michael to reply but continues speaking.

'Well, 'spect you've read about what's going on over there, with the Jerries getting the upper hand and all that.'

'I've seen it in the papers,' replies Michael matter-of-factly.

'Well, I've been told there's a special job going on and it's tomorrow,' replies George.

'What kind of special job?'

'Well, I've been told the advancing German Army has trapped the British and French armies on the beaches around Dunkirk. Around 330,000 troops are there, and it's up to us to get them out of it.'

'That many!' Michael tries to imagine this number of men all pouring on to Dunkirk's beaches, but it is impossible. His mind can't take it in.

'Yes, that many,' replies George simply. 'For some reason, and no one knows why, Hitler has demanded a pause in the fighting and it has given the Allies the chance to evacuate from Dunkirk.'

'So what do you mean, it's up to us? What about the Navy?'

'The Navy can't get in, no large boat can get near the men.'

'How do you mean?'

'The Dunkirk beaches are on such a shallow slope. And it's bad, real bad.'

'Oh, right, I see what you mean; but where do we come in?' Michael replies, rubbing his chin, a habit he has when listening to something important. He is aware it is a rather non-committal answer, but then there are times when he finds it hard to express his emotions verbally.

'Smaller boats are needed to take the men on board and then they will be transferred to larger boats based further offshore.'

'I'm with you so far,' replies Michael.

'So the powers that be,' continues George in a fast voice, 'want those of us who own small boats and those with pleasure boats, private yachts and launches moored on the River Thames to go to Dunkirk and bring our chaps home.'

Michael doesn't reply. He senses what is coming next. His hands begin to feel damp with tiny trickles of sweat. He unconsciously rubs them on his shirt sleeves.

'Mickey, my lad,' George continues. 'I want you to come with me to Dunkirk. I can skipper the boat and you know the ropes as good as me, and I'm thinking of a third; you and I are not getting any younger.'

He sees Michael's face pale at the enormity of what he has just heard. The war out there has suddenly become very personal for both of them.

'You can say no and I won't hold it against you.' George looks earnestly at his friend. For a few moments Michael doesn't speak. The enormity of what he has just heard is still sinking in.

A picture of his twin lads comes to mind again. They sacrificed their own lives allowing him to grow old. He must go, if only for their sakes. After all, he has had a good life. Then, looking his friend in the eye, very slowly, he nods. George understands the nod.

'So who is going to be our third, then?'

'I thought maybe Jimmy,' replies George.

'What, are you mad? You know about Jimmy, don't you?' exclaims Michael.

'Let's forget about him being... well... what he is. I've seen him in the shop and he's got the three main characteristics of being a good soldier.'

'Oh, I know who you're thinking of now – Old Joe who used to come in to the pub and talk all the time about the last war and what makes a good soldier.'

Michael smiles ruefully at the memory of the old veteran they used to know.

'Yes, and what did he say?' asks George.

'Don't remind me, I can say it off by heart. The three fs – fidelity, focus and follow orders!'

'So, then, Mickey lad, let's take them one at a time, like Old Joe did. One – fidelity. Jimmy's loyal. Look how hard he works for you in the shop. Two – focus. He's got an eye for detail. Look how he stacks things perfectly straight. Three – follow orders. He does what he's told, you can't deny it; he wants to please you. Plus he's got the strength of an ox, and it's what our lads over there need the most now.'

Michael becomes quiet again. He can understand the sense of what his friend is saying. Jimmy is younger and stronger than both of them, but the thought of involving him in the war appals him. He looks at his friend, who is eagerly waiting for an answer. He cannot say no; George is right, there are soldiers over the sea, just a few short miles away, that need people with the kind of strength Jimmy has.

'Well, yes, I suppose you're right. I can see what you mean, but heaven only knows what Frieda will say about all of this.'

Actually, he has a jolly good idea what she will say about it, and he senses it isn't going to be easy.

'Well, what's up? You said nothing through tea. You've got a face like a wet weekend. Either you've done something wrong or you're hiding something.'

Frieda scrutinises her husband's face as if the truth is written there upon it. They are sitting together in their small sitting room. Meg has gone home and Jimmy is having a bath.

'It's about the war. And I'm warning you now, it might shock you.'

Michael then relates the conversation he had with George earlier that day, but omits the bit at the end about Jimmy. He doesn't stop for breath to prevent interruptions from his wife. She tries to protest her concern about her husband's safety without success. It has been one of the longest speeches he has made in a long time. He stops and waits for the storm to begin. It comes in one explosive blast.

'Are you mad!'

'Frieda love, listen, there's more. It's tomorrow.'

'Tomorrow!'

'Yes, we assemble together here in Dover. It will be us and a flotilla of small vessels setting out to cross the Channel. Frieda, love...' he pauses. 'I have to do it for our boys...' he pauses again, this time for longer. 'And there's something else I need to tell you about. George says we need a third man on the boat. Well, we're getting on a bit and we need someone who is young and strong to help us.'

Frieda doesn't reply. She is puzzled as to whom George can be referring to.

'And,' continues Michael, 'George wants Jimmy to be that man.'

Michael stops speaking and waits for the next explosion. He doesn't have to wait long.

'What, Jimmy, our Jimmy? The man's mad! Does he know what Jimmy is? Well, I don't want to sound unkind, but people like Jimmy don't go to war!'

'I know, I said roughly the same thing myself. Anyway, I was going to say he noticed how strong Jimmy is when he was helping to carry boxes of supplies for me and how loyal he is and so on. And I can't deny it. And look, love, our lads over there – well, it's not the chaps with degrees in goodness knows what that they need. What they really need now are people who are strong, like Jimmy. And shouldn't we give him a chance to serve his country?'

He has said it all. It has been a speech equal to Churchill himself. He waits for the next barrage of words. It doesn't come. Frieda is now silent. Then after a few moments she speaks.

'I'm thinking it shouldn't be us that decides. Mary brought him here; it should be Mary who decides.'

'Do you think she's well enough, with the high blood pressure and everything?' asks Michael.

'I think we have to take that risk. Supposing Jimmy got hurt, or worse?' She couldn't bring herself to say the word 'dies'. 'Then how would Mary feel, knowing we sent him off to war without telling her? No, it has to be her decision and only hers.'

'Then that's what we'll do. So be it.'

It is a short drive to the hospital and they arrive in good time. It is easy to find the right ward as Frieda knows it well. A number of visitors are gathering outside the ward, mostly

223

nervous grandmas-to-be and female siblings. There are very few dads, just some who have reserved occupations. The door to the ward opens and a small plump woman wearing a blue uniform appears.

'Visiting time is strictly one hour, and mind you don't overexcite the patients.'

They enter the ward in one mass of legs and arms and then separate out to seek their own relations. They find them easily enough. Each mother-to-be is sitting up straight with two equal-placed pillows supporting their upper backs and necks. Each is proudly bearing a bump in various sizes under pristine white hospital sheets and straightened yellow and blue blankets.

'There she is, Michael, where she was last time I came, second to the end on the left.'

'Oh yes.'

They walk to Mary's bed. She is looking surprised to see her uncle with Auntie Frieda. Michael speaks first.

'Hello, Mary, love, sorry I haven't...'

'It's fine, Uncle, really it is. It's a bit, well, embarrassing for men. You're looking well.'

Her attempt to put her uncle at his ease produces a smile from him and a quick kiss on the forehead.

Frieda then hugs Mary.

'How are you, love?' Frieda asks.

'Bored out of my mind,' answers Mary, glancing at Michael who is now studying his feet intensely. She continues hurriedly, 'but the medical stuff is fine, thank goodness. They're going to let me out soon. Oh, and about the fig rolls.' Mary's words end in a giggle.

She is thinking about the six packets of fig rolls she has in her locker, chosen by Jimmy to give to Frieda for her. Frieda has tried to get Jimmy to give something different but it had to be fig rolls. Neither of them knows why.

Frieda paints a tiny smile on her face but doesn't reply. She is thinking about what she is going to say to Mary about Jimmy. There is an uncomfortable silence for a few moments.

'Anything wrong, Auntie Frieda?'

'Well, love, we have something to say to you about Jimmy.'

'No, Frieda,' Michael interrupts firmly. 'I have, it has to be me.'

Michael tells her all about Dunkirk and the possibility of taking Jimmy with him.

Mary listens without interrupting but doesn't reply straightaway. She is seeing a piture-memory in her mind of a young man singing 'Old MacDonald Had a Farm'. She is remembering how she had connected with him that day. She had felt protective and motherly. And now the decision to protect him once more has come her way. They are looking at her, waiting for her answer, what is she to say?

Suddenly the ward door bangs open and a small boy bursts in with an adult in tow behind him who could be his grandma.

'Mummy!' he bellows.

He is wearing callipers which are supporting his stick-like wasted legs. But they do not stop him from hobbling purposefully towards the bed where Mummy is.

Expectant mums begin staring. Some are muttering to their visitors. Some are looking ashamed of the comments they have just made. Others are simply afraid.

What must it be like to cope with a child who is crippled for life? they think. How will their own unborn children play if they are not able to run about? Would polio affect any of their other children? It is the disease that so many mothers dread. It is a killer disease; it cuts the heart out of so many families.

'Mummy!' he hollers again. He arrives at her bed and throws himself in to her waiting arms.

'This is my Tommy, everyone. I know what you're thinking because I thought it too. I was afraid when he got polio, but then Tommy taught me how to stop being afraid. He is teaching me how to love. When you love like he does, you stop worrying about the future. You live for each moment. That's all I have to say.'

Everyone is quiet now, waiting for the first person to say something. It is an uncomfortable silence. Then a little voice speaks.

'I dids a pitshure for you, Mummy.'

'Aw, bless im.'

The atmosphere changes in a second. Tommy's simple statement has done it, and visitors begin to speak again. Frieda then takes hold of Mary's hand. She has decided it is now time for a decision.

'So, Mary, love, do we allow Jimmy to go to Dunkirk?'

'I think,' Mary replies, 'that Tommy here has shown us the answer. Jimmy is teaching us how to love. Oh, we thought we knew all about love, at least I thought I did, but Jimmy has shown us what real love is. I know he will say yes because he truly believes his grandma is behind the sea. I didn't know until you told me, and it explains everything. We have to let him look for his own love answer. It's hard for us, but we have to let him go.'

'Are you sure?'

'Yes.'

And now there are no more words left to say. The enormity of Dunkirk is ahead of them, and Jimmy may well be a part of it all.

Neither of them sleep well that night. The clock on the bedside table becomes the most watched clock in Dover. When Michael wakes up in the night his immediate thoughts are about Jimmy. What is he going to say to him in the morning?

When Frieda wakes it is after disturbing, incoherent dreams. In one of then she is rescuing Michael from the mouth of a dragon which turns out to be a whale. In another she is baling out a boat full of seawater with a kettle. The kettle begins to speak and it is then she realises that Michael is asking if he should put the kettle on, and in fact she is waking up.

'Cup of tea, love?'

'Yes, thanks,' replies a sleepy Frieda. It seems strange to them both that they are speaking in such an ordinary way.

'You were tossing and turning. I reckon you are all at sea!' Michael smiles at the irony of his words.

'You can say that again.'

'Snuggle down; I'll be back in a jiff.'

Michael gets out of bed and goes downstairs to the kitchen. He returns with a tray of two cups and saucers from their best tea set, a pot of tea, a jug of milk and some sugar in a bowl from the same set. He sets it down on their bedside table and pours the tea, adds the milk and puts one teaspoonful of sugar in his own cup. He then hands Frieda hers and takes his own.

Frieda smiles at the sight of it all despite the seriousness of their situation. She is remembering how they chose the pattern together, a wedding present from her mother. She knows Michael is now trying to comfort her with a shared memory.

They sip their tea and for a few moments neither of them speaks.

Michael takes one more sip of tea, the last in the cup. Dawn is now lighting their bedroom and bringing back to life its simple bits of furniture. His eyes rest on the brass-framed wedding photograph of them both, proudly displayed in centre position on the dressing table. They had been so young, so hopeful of a future together. They had survived the last war and now war has come again – and it wants him. This is the surprise it has handed out.

'You're going to ask him properly, aren't you, Jimmy I mean, like, man to man?'

'Yes,' replies Michael gently.

'And will you...'

He stops her words with one finger on her lips. He doesn't want words now; he wants love. He needs to hold her. It could be the last time. He takes her in his arms...

A tender love joins them together as husband and wife. It has been a long time since they have known that level of intimacy with each other.

Michael is now looking at Jimmy. There are just the two of them. The older man and the younger one, divided only by age. Frieda isn't there. She told Michael earlier that she doesn't want to be there when he asks Jimmy to go to Dunkirk. Michael has agreed and now he is thinking of what to say. He studies the young man in front of him: Jimmy, whom he has only known a short time. What does he really know about him? How much does he know about war, if anything at all?

Here he is, a young Geordie lad with the muscles of a grown man but with an innocent child-like heart. And he is planning to take him to war. Is he doing the right thing? Is he being cruel? Supposing he is killed? How is he to face not just Frieda, but Mary and Meg as well, and tell them the news that Jimmy isn't coming home? Then, of course, George and he might be killed; how will Jimmy cope with that?

He feels a surge of nausea wave through his stomach. But there are so many out there who depend on help arriving soon. It is worse for them, those who are the casualties of war, and it is about the outcome of the war too. These men have to get away; they have to find the strength to return to fight again. And it is up to Great Britain to make sure the job is done properly.

And now it is up to him to say it in a way that Jimmy understands. No school examination is as tough as this. He will have to take this slowly in the hope that the lad will understand it all. Taking one deep slow breath, he begins.

'Jimmy, listen, I have a special job for you.'

He pauses for a second and then goes on.

'Jimmy, I want you to come with me on a boat.' He pauses again before continuing. 'Can you tell me if you want to come?'

Jimmy's mind is now processing the words he has just heard. There are a lot of them together. Some of them disappear around a corner in his head but the words 'boat' and 'want to come' spring up and fizz in his mind.

Jimmy go on a boat.

His mind sings the word **'boat'** to him and the song makes him jump one happy jump in the air.

Michael knows this means yes, but he must keep going.

'And Jimmy, the boat will be on the sea.'

A boat on the sea.

The effect of the words 'the sea' is immediate. They are the last two words in the sentence and they wave into Jimmy's head with one big, very bright, purple wave. And he jumps with them two happy jumps.

And then the most glorious words he has ever heard sound in his head. They smile a big purple smile:

Jimmy see Grandma.

Jimmy cuddle Grandma.

JIMMY CUDDLE GRANDMA BEHIND THE SEA.

At last the time has come. It is the time he will go behind the sea and find Grandma. And because he is the happiest he has been for a long time, he jumps three of the biggest toe-springing jumps he has ever done.

'Now, Jimmy, we will be going across the sea.'

And once more Jimmy jumps at the word 'sea'.

'And Jimmy, we will be helping some men who are sad.'

Jimmy likes the word 'help' as he has helped Grandma lots of times in the hoose. He claps his hands three times.

'And Jimmy, the men might be hurt too.'

This time there is no response from Jimmy. Michael tries a different tactic.

'But Jimmy, we can help them get better. We can bring them home.'

This time the effect is immediate. Jimmy has understood the word 'better'. Maybe Grandma has gone behind the sea to help the hurt men. The other words he has heard now slip away, but 'better' is an important word. So he jumps his 'yes-answer' yet again.

So far Michael and Jimmy have understood each other, but Michael feels he must be honest with the lad. He must warn him there can be risks to his own safety.

'And Jimmy, you might get hurt too.'

For Jimmy, the word 'hurt' is a bad word. It is red, loud and bloodied.

Jimmy not like hurt.

He looks down at his feet, then his legs, then up to his chest as far as his eyes can see. He doesn't want any of the things he can see to get hurt. He can see they aren't hurt now and that is a relief. He goes very quiet. He can't jump now. He can't clap now. He doesn't know what he is supposed to do, and for a few moments his mind goes blank. Michael is wise enough not to break the silence. The tension in the room is palpable.

Then something strange happens to Jimmy. It is as though Grandma is in the room standing next to him. He feels her hand touch his shoulder. It is a light, gentle touch. He isn't frightened and a flush of calmness soothes the inside of his head. Familiar words of long ago begin to form in his mind, or is it recently? He can't remember. They are words which Grandma used to say to him when she wanted him to do something. Then slowly they come back to him and repeat themselves three times.

Jimmy be a good boy now. Jimmy be a good boy now. Jimmy be a good boy now.

He so wants to be a good boy for Grandma but the red hurt word he has just heard hasn't gone away. What is he to do? Then once more he hears the purple song, but this time it is soothing and quieter.

Jimmy be a good boy now.

But the song is also compelling in its quietness with a gentle authority that Jimmy understands. He knows he has to obey it. And for the first time in his life he knows he has to face the blood. The boy Jimmy has become a man. It is a feeling he can't put into words, but he knows something special has happened to him and now, what to do next? What is it he did when he heard Grandma's good-boy words? He thinks hard. Then he remembers.

Jimmy not rush.

Very slowly he looks for his coat and puts it on. Then he walks very slowly to the door and waits. Michael has been watching Jimmy all the time he has been silent, not taking his eyes off his face. And now, seeing Jimmy's deliberate movement towards the door he takes this as a 'yes' and walks to the door too. Then he reaches out and takes hold of Jimmy's hand and shakes it three times. And now the day lies in front of them with a host of question marks as to what they might experience in Dunkirk.

CHAPTER
20

Wednesday, 29 May 1940

Jimmy can't take in all he is seeing. He is on a boat on the sea, surrounded by other boats. Some are the same size as the one he is on and some are bigger. There are lots of them and Jimmy wonders if they are all going to bring the hurt men home. He has met the George man and shaken his hand three times. The George man smiled at him and Jimmy noticed he had three teeth missing on the top row. Jimmy had wondered if he had swallowed them.

It is going to be a good day and now he is experiencing the sea close up with all its power. He has seen it and marvelled at it and now he can touch and smell it. He can't describe the smell; it is something new; but it makes his body tingle with vitality. Today he will find Grandma. It is as good a day as the Sunday church morning days. His special broken morning song begins to sing and fill his head.

He looks at the mountains behind him. He likes them because they are white. He wonders if the black bits in them are long bits of coal. He wonders if the Frieda lady has dug some of them out for the sitting room fire.

He looks at the big white birds that are making croaking noises as they drop and push up their bodies. He sees them disappear in the waves only to come out again with food in their mouths. He wonders how they know where the food is.

But the best thing is the music of the sea. To Jimmy it has its own tune with words that belong only to itself. It changes as the wind moves the water around and up and down. It whooshes in his ears, filling them up. It breathes with him, its pulse waves with his own. It rocks him up near to the sky. It is a feeling he has never felt before. It makes him feel happy and he wants to jump three happy jumps, but he mustn't. The boat has begun moving and he doesn't want to jump in to the sea. He doesn't want to squash the fish.

Instead he counts the people in the boat. He counts himself first: that makes one man, Jimmy. Then he counts the Michael man; that makes two. Then he counts the George man; that makes three. Three people in the boat; and there is a lot of floor in the boat. That means there is floor for Grandma to sit on when she comes back from being behind the sea.

And now Jimmy feels as though he has all the time in the world. He feels free, as though nothing can ever trouble him again. He feels as though he is in church and lots of people are going to sleep on their knees. Is it this or the rocking of the boat that makes him sleep? He doesn't know, but when he awakes it is to a very different sea and a very different smell.

It is the smell that wakes him up. It is going up his nose and down all of his body. It is keeping his eyes closed. It is a bad smell and it brings back a bad memory. The smell reminds him of rotten bird eggs and the sky sparking with burning red darts. When was it? Then the smell gives him a picture in his head. It is him, Jimmy, walking to the bumwoodhole at the bottom of the garden at the hoose he shared with Grandma. The picture in his head has unwound itself. He is back in his garden wearing his pyjamas. He is hearing a big bad noise and it is making him fly through the air. Now he is falling down to earth again and the roof of the bumwoodhole is rising up to his head. A pain is shaking through his body in a sickening thud. And now bad red words are shouting in his head.

Jimmy body not right. Jimmy body not right. Not right not right.

He shakes his head quickly to get rid of them. The memories blur into one horrible, bloodied mess – but they won't go away. He can feel the boat slowing down. He must open his eyes to let the memories out of his head. He must open them wide so they will all go together.

When Jimmy opens his eyes it is to an evil he could never imagine. This is the moment when everyone on the boat sees together for the first time the reality of what they have come to.

The sight that meets them convulses their bodies with shock and silences them to stone. Whatever idea they may have had about what awaits them is taken away in a moment. The destruction they are now witnessing has devastated this part of northern France. Whenever the weather has allowed, the Luftwaffe has attacked Dunkirk, reducing the town to rubble. The harbour has been destroyed by heavy German bombing and a huge fire is raging out of control and belching thick, acrid smoke.

But worst of all is the sight of hundreds of thousands of men on the beach, hoping to be rescued. As well as the British Expeditionary Force, there are French and Belgian refugees too. All of them have one simple hope: to get to England and freedom.

They have experienced the worse kind of defeat possible; the knowledge that they have failed to stop the terrible advance of the enemy. Each man has been swamped by despair. They are exhausted, hungry and in some cases suffering terrible injuries. Many have died horribly of their wounds. Each man is queuing patiently, taking his turn to wade out into the open sea towards the big ships. Each is hoping and praying that he will be one of those who will make it this time.

To add to this there is the constant attack from machine-gun fire and enemy bombing.

All Jimmy can see now are the wasp-like sting colours of yellow and black. It is the sting of something very bad and he doesn't understand what it is. Then for the second time in his life Jimmy feels anger. He has experienced it on the train for a moment, but now the anger is taking him over. The men who have made this happen must be bad men.

The bad men must not do it again. Jimmy will help the good men. Grandma will help the good men too. His eyes widen as he takes in the scene in front of him. It is now one panoramic view and he can see everything. He is behind the sea. Grandma must be here. His eyes scan everything he can see. He looks up and down and sideways and turns round and looks behind him – but she isn't there. He knows she isn't playing the hide-and-seek game as she has always said he has to be happy before they can play it – and he certainly isn't happy now.

He had expected her to be where he could see her.
She isn't there.

Grandma gone?

Jimmy hasn't been aware of Michael watching him. Michael
has witnessed everything and his heart now lurches within him.
It is time Jimmy knows the truth.

'She's not here, Jimmy. She's deaded, when the hoose went
bang.'

He knows his words sound brutal, but he also knows there
is no other way to say it.

Deaded. Deaded. DEADED?

The words explode in Jimmy's brain. This is his nemesis. He
will never see Grandma again? Is this true? Michael sees the
question appear in Jimmy eyes. It cuts him to the heart.

'Jimmy, I don't like saying this, but she became deaded when
the hoose went bang.'

Grandma deaded.

This is the moment when the happy sea film ends. The truth
blasts through his brain in red blood grief. It pierces his very
being. He wants to shout out NO but his mouth won't open.
The shock immobilises him.

Memories of words and things he has seen – Mrs Bailey's
tipsy words, the policeman's body in bits, the wide-open eyes of
Old Doug – all come together in a jigsaw pattern. Even a tinge
of a memory of the church when Grandma tried to show him
what happened to her is coming back. Grandma is deaded; he

237

will never see her again. She is not behind the sea. There will be no more cuddles and wet cat holes. No more plum jam and rhubarb pie. No more angels in church and no more singing.

The utter desolation of it all overwhelms him. He shuts his eyes tight in the hope it will all go away; but when he opens them it is still here.

He wants to be deaded too; even being deaded will be better than the grief he now feels; but the waves of the sea will not let him go. They are determined to move him forwards. It is as though he is the only person in the world who is driven by them. His world by now has shrunk to a narrow tunnel and he is being forced down it. He is totally unaware of anything or anybody around him. It is just him and the sounds and the hideous rhythms of pain and death.

And all of it is coming nearer, and with it a smell that is familiar. He thinks for a while... when has he smelt it before? The smell is rushing down his nose and entering his body. Then his memory rewinds itself again and a ghastly picture begins to come into focus, a rabbit, a dead rabbit with crawly things going in to its mouth and body.

It is too much for him. He shuts his body in to a tight ball and locks himself against the side of the boat. He will never come out, never again.

Jimmy not come back, never never NEVER.

The happy morning has turned into the worst day of Jimmy's life.

CHAPTER
21

'How many will fit in the boat safely?' Michael's pragmatic question breaks the nerve-racking silence that has now settled in the boat. He must stay focused. His voice sounds as though it is coming from a long way off. But he is determined not to let his nerves show.

'About fifteen, I reckon.' George's voice holds a tremor. It isn't what he was about to say but he keeps the expletives to himself. He had not expected it to be this bad. Instead he kicks the side of the boat hard with his right foot. Unlike his friend, he is used to expressing his feelings. Turning to Michael he speaks again.

'Right, then, let's get em in.' His voice has steadied a little.

Michael looks at Jimmy and speaks.

'Jimmy, look up. Jimmy, there are hurted men here. Jimmy, you can help them. Jimmy, will you help them?'

No answer.

'Jimmy, I think Grandma would want you to help the hurted men.'

Jimmy hears the words Michael says. He has heard all of the words spoken. They have come down at him and gone in to his ears. They have made sense. He has to make a decision. There are no colour words or films to help him; it is up to him now.

The boat has brought him here and he has learnt that Grandma is deaded. And it has been a huge shock. But now something new is happening. The picture of hurted men he has seen fills his mind and leaves no room for anything else. He has to get them in the boat. He has to stop fifteen men from being deaded.

He glances quickly at his hands and arms still curled up They have changed. They are bigger and stronger. The wobbly boy-flesh has firmed up in to muscle. He now has the strong hands and arms of a man.

A new energy begins to rush through them.

Then suddenly, to the surprise of the other two men, he jumps up in the air and down into the shallow sea. The shock of the cold water against his legs makes him gasp but there is no time to lose. Deaded may be waiting for them all. Deaded might get them like it got Grandma. He races towards the shore. Meg's words come in to his mind as he runs: 'Yer needs to look, Jimmy. Jimmy, yer needs to look at the eyes.'

Then the picture of the Doug man comes in his head and how the little hair-eye bits that move up and down did not work any more. He has to get to the hurted men before that happens.

It only takes a few seconds to reach the shore. His legs still feel cold but he has to find the lying-down men and look at their eyes. He has to find the men whose eyes haven't gone dark. He has to take them to the Michael and George mens.

Different queues of men are now wading out to sea to waiting boats but Jimmy doesn't see them. The tunnel he is now in has just one man at the end of it. He is lying down, curled up in a tight ball with his head bent down towards his chest. Jimmy runs towards him. He must get to the man before deaded does. He must run as fast as he can. He gets there. He bends down to see his eyes. He bends his head as close as he can. Thick yellow-black smoke is making his eyes sting and he rubs them to make the sting go away. It doesn't. He must lay his chin on the hurted man's face, as close as he can, so he can see the little eye-hairs. He can see them, they are moving! The man isn't deaded. He must pull with his arms. He must pull the man towards the sea and the boat. He must go back and get another one.

Back in the boat, Michael and George stand mesmerised for a few seconds. Then Michael realises what Jimmy is doing. He is ignoring the walking wounded men and selecting those who cannot walk. A rescue-relay plan comes into his head.

'Right, then, George, you stay in the boat. I'll wade half way out and meet Jimmy and take over. Then you can haul them in.'

The plan works. They get seven wounded men on the boat; each time Jimmy selects them by observing their eyes. Some men from the wading queue have also managed to get on the boat by hauling themselves on, but Jimmy hasn't seen them. His tunnel has remained. The number fifteen is etched on his brain.

But the effort of it all is now showing in Jimmy's movements. He is determined to rescue fifteen men. He has kept count on his fingers but it is getting harder all the

241

time. Sweat is pouring down him and is mingling with blood from other men's bodies, staining the sea around him in red, bloodied pools.

His eyes have blurred one fraction more with each rescue, but he knows he must go on. Men are shouting in words he doesn't understand. French, Belgian and Dutch voices blend with English ones. But Jimmy knows nothing about nationality; he has to find the next hurted man and get him to the boat.

He glances down at his fingers: the image is now completely blurred, making some fingers look as if there is a shadow behind them. He feels for his thumb, and feeling each finger and remaining thumb in turn, he counts to nine. Then, clutching his hands together, he runs once more to the beach.

Suddenly he hears what he thinks is someone calling his name. It is coming a little way onto the beach. It is faint, but it is there. Who can be calling him? He hears it again, a man's voice – weak, but one he has heard before. He runs towards it and then he sees the man who is calling his name. He is lying flat on his back, his rifle beside him, staring at the sky. Blood is pouring from an open-leg fracture and the bone is twisted horrendously at a strange angle. But his vision is clear and he has seen Jimmy and recognised him straightaway.

Jimmy bends down to see who it is. His eyes are now very blurred. He wipes them with the back of his hand; it makes little difference, but just enough to see the man's eyes. The shock of who it is makes him jump involuntarily. He is staring into the eyes of the Ian man.

'Help me, Jimmy. I know I was bad to you, but for Pete's sake get me out of here.'

Jimmy stares at the Ian man not quite knowing what to do. The hate-cold eyes he saw for the first time at the farm now have a different look in them. They are helpless, pleading and begging for help. He stops; part of him wants to find someone else to rescue, but he can't move away. He has grown up into a man. He has a choice now, which is it to be? Large drops of sweat are now dripping down his face. He has never felt anguish like this before. It fills his head.

He begins to feel his hands move towards the Ian man. No, the Ian man is a bad man. He jerks them back to his chest but they are so heavy now, he must let them go to sleep. He must put them on his legs. Then he hears a noise. It is a noise he has heard before. It is the same noise he heard when the policeman had been chasing him. Michael and George have heard it too.

'Run, Jimmy, run!' yells Michael.

He must get away, he must save his legs from being deaded. He must save his arms from being deaded. He must save the Ian man from getting deaded. He must be good. He must stop all the deading.

Grabbing hold of Ian's arms, he pulls them with all the remaining strength he has left and runs for the sea. The noise of the plane is getting louder and drowning out Ian's moans. Men dive for cover, throwing themselves down behind anything which might protect them. A dog screams its terror.

It is no good; Jimmy's legs give way under him. Hunger and exhaustion have finally got to him. He struggles to get up, but in doing so he lets go of Ian's arms. Ian has managed to keep his head out of the water but now is too weak to do so. Michael, seeing the soldier might drown, runs towards him and pulls him onto the boat.

'Run, Jimmy!' bellows Michael.

Jimmy tries to stand up but his body is too weak to move.

It is all over in a moment. The explosion yellows all around him, then blackness.

CHAPTER
22

The rescued men on the boat see it all. Jimmy is dead. There will be no funeral, no coffin, and no spring flowers on a grave. There is nothing now but Michael's spat out curse words in the sky. They fall. The reddening sea spurts them back.

They are the only words spoken from a boat now filled with injured soldiers. Michael's words have said it all.

There is nothing they can do but go home.

As they leave, Michael's vomit mixes with Jimmy's word-red blood in the death waves of the sea. A hideous gut mess splashes itself in to the bloodied shore and joins a carnage of human destruction.

There will be more to come, but not for Michael's eyes to see.

It's hard to describe how Frieda feels when she hears the news about Jimmy or to count the number of tears she shed. But eventually the sobs cease and as she lies next to her husband in bed she feels the urge to pray. It has been a long time since she has prayed but now she knows she has to. A whisper memory of a prayer she chanted as a child at Sunday school comes in to her mind. She remembers how thrilled she was to receive her first Book of Common Prayer, given to her from her auntie, as a present at her first communion.

> *Our Father who art in heaven,*
> *hallowed be thy name.*
> *Thy kingdom come.*
> *Thy will be done*
> *on earth as it is in heaven.*
> *Give us this day our daily bread,*
> *and forgive us our trespasses,*
> *as we forgive those who trespass*
> *against us,*
> *and lead us not into temptation,*
> *but deliver us from evil.*
> *For thine is the kingdom,*
> *and the power, and the glory,*
> *for ever and ever.*
> *Amen*

When she gets to the end she hears Michael whisper, 'Amen.' It is there, a croaked whisper, but there is no mistaking it.

'I thought you'd gone to sleep.'

'No, I was just thinking. You could say when the light went out of his eyes he became what he is destined to be, a hero.'

'Yes, but I think it is more than that,' replies Frieda. 'He became Jimmy, the man he was meant to be.'

She doesn't know when she went to sleep or when she started to dream, but it is a dream like no other she has dreamt before. She is in a still, silent place and the light around her sparkles with a hue which is not of this earth. She doesn't feel she is dreaming as everything around her seems to pulsate with energy and vibrancy. In front of her is the sea; but this is no death scene. And there is Jimmy as she has known him. And walking towards him is an old lady with a crinkled face, wearing a pinny which is loosening around her waist.

Then Frieda wakes up. Early morning sunshine is peeping shyly through the bedroom curtains and a dawn bird is singing. The happy song reminds her of the hymn Meg had been singing lately in the shop. She smiles ruefully at the memory of Meg's own version.

Morning is broken!
Liker new morning!
Blackburd has spokes on!
Like the first bird.

Michael, the husband she loves completely, has come back to her. Jimmy hasn't. She will never see him again; but as she lies there she knows for certain that he has found Grandma behind the sea.

END NOTE

In a few days' time the Prime Minister, Winston Churchill, will describe the 'miracle of deliverance' from Dunkirk and warn of an impending invasion. He is careful not to describe this deliverance as a victory as 'Wars are not won by evacuations'.

His moving speech to Parliament will come on the day the last Allied soldier will arrive home from France at the end of a ten-day operation to bring back hundreds of thousands of retreating Allied troops, trapped by the German Army.

This is a section from that speech:

We shall go on to the end, we shall fight in France,
we shall fight on the seas and oceans,
we shall fight with growing confidence and growing strength in the
air, we shall defend our island, whatever the cost may be.
We shall fight on the beaches,
we shall fight on the landing grounds,
we shall fight in the fields and in the streets,
we shall fight in the hills;
we shall never surrender, and even if, which I do not for a moment
believe, this island or a large part of it were subjugated and starving,
then our Empire beyond the seas, armed and guarded by the British

fleet, would carry on the struggle, until, in God's good time, the New World, with all its power and might, steps forth to the rescue and the liberation of the old.

At the beginning, it was hoped that 45,000 men might be evacuated. In reality, over 338,000 Allied troops reached England, including 26,000 French soldiers.

Without the 'little ships', only a fraction of the troops would have been transported from the beaches. The nation prayed its tender prayers and those prayers were answered. It is indeed a miracle of deliverance.

Lightning Source UK Ltd.
Milton Keynes UK
UKOW02f0852010916

281971UK00002B/38/P